BEATING TO WINDWARD

A voyage

in the *Gloucester Daily Times* through

the stormy years from 1967 to 1973

Joseph E. Garland

THE CURIOUS TRAVELLER PRESS
Gloucester, Massachusetts 01930

THE CURIOUS TRAVELLER PRESS
a division of
The Pressroom, Incorporated
32 Blackburn Center
Gloucester, Massachusetts 01930

Printed in the United States of America

ISBN 09625660-1-2

Designed by Inga Soderberg

These articles were originally printed in the
Gloucester Daily Times *and are reprinted with permission.*

Picture Credits
Cover, Helen Garland photo; 17 Sawyer Free Library; 35 author;
36 Cape Ann Historical Association; 41 Doris McPhee Martell;
42 *Out of Gloucester*, James B. Connolly; 46 Doris McPhee Martell;
55, 56, 59 *North Shore '71*; 62, 69 author's collection; 70 author;
72 *The Real McCoy*, Bill McCoy; 81 author; 83 James E. Brennan;
88 *North Shore '72*; 91 author's collection; 96 Charles F. Sayle collection;
108 Charles A. Lowe photo; 109 author; 111 author's collection;
112 author; 118 author (after Audubon); 132 *Gloucester Daily Times*;
136 Ernest L. Blatchford photo, Cape Ann Historical Association;
143 Charles A. Lowe photo; 145 author; back cover, Charles A. Lowe photo.

To the exuberant memory of

Phil Weld

Sailor, soldier, scholar and gentleman

Newspaper guy

who brought good journalism back to Cape Ann

Fast friend,

and above all,

joyful lover of life

CONTENTS ~w~

PREFACE ~~~

FEW NEWSPAPER COLUMNS OUTLAST THE YELLOWING PAGE, FEWER STILL THE deadlined columnist who strives on demand to fish something wise, withering, witty. whimsical or wistful from the onrushing daily stream.

On the other hand, I'm pleased to rationalize, more often than not I wrung as much sweat, word for word and fish for fish, from fashioning most of the 350 columns that appeared off and on in the *Gloucester Daily Times* across twenty-four years as from any of fourteen-odd books. So shucks, why not a bookful of them?

It had started in that Vietnam-torn year of 1967. I was in the 'tweenbooks doldrums and in November SOSed my old friend from post-WWII newspaper days in Boston and eye-to-eye neighbor across Gloucester Harbor, Phil Weld, great single-handed transatlantic sailor-to-be, and owner of the *Times*.

Adrift, I threw him a line: How's about I do a column "trying to get at some of the essence of Gloucester and its uniqueness, its great maritime traditions, people past and present and so on, with comments on current matters as one is moved?"

Phil took me in tow. Those were terrible years of turmoil and tragedy. As an old soldier, a writer of liberal persuasion, a former newsman, I tried to come to grips with troubling issues, speaking out, reminding myself and my neighbors of what struck me as good and solid and enduring, and representing a consistent point of view at least when all around was turbulence. Hence, "Beating to Windward with Joe Garland."

As I got back to bookwriting, the twice-weekly pace fell off to weekly. When the late Paul Kenyon, Nestor of the *Times*, long its anonymous "Lookout", and the best editor I ever had, launched the Essex County

Newspapers' weekly *North Shore '70*, he brought me with him until even that agreeable spot proved too much to fill, and in 1973 I departed the newspaper business for the second time, returning to the *Times* as a columnist again from 1988 to 1991.

When Dave McAveeney, owner of The Pressroom, who had printed my new edition of "The Gloucester Guide" for Protean Press of Rockport in l990, suggested that we do something else, I suggested some of the first run of columns. I was astonished when he went for the idea — pig, poke and all.

So thanks to Dave and his amiable crew up in Blackburn Park for enabling this reunion of scribbler and scribbles, and to Peter Watson, General Manager of Essex County Newspapers, and Mary Wessling Harrington, Editor of the *Gloucester Daily Times*, and her staff for their friendly support and cooperation.

A tip of the cap in fond memory of Phil Weld, Paul Kenyon and Billy Cahill, a trio of old-fashioned, fire-chasing, hot-lead, pencil-stub, back-of-the-envelope newsmen in the old tradition.

A salute to my late father and lifelong mentor, Doctor Joe, who in 1930 put out a collection of his early columns in *The New England Journal of Medicine* of which he was later the distinguished Editor. "The Doctor's Saddle-Bag" contained a literary mix as varied and therapeutic as the remedies that both his medical grandfather and father carried on their rounds of Gloucester between 1849 and 1907.

And to Helen for her amused "Why not?"

Joe Garland
Black Bess, Eastern Point
July 1994

Bound Out

1. A SQUARE PEG AND A ROUND HOLE ⚊ⱯⱲ⚊

AFTER WASTING THE BETTER PART OF a day bent over a hot typewriter, I am about ready to conclude that the first column, like the first batch of pancakes, should be thrown out.

The trouble is that the frying pan isn't just right yet, and the fire ain't either, and since I expect from here on to be in one or the other, I'd like a little more time in the galley to get the seat of my britches used to the heat before slinging the grub along.

But to scrap the first column before it was fairly begun, like leaving out the 13th floor in the skyscraper, would be the coward's way. What shred of conscience I have left, therefore, makes me write this as a hint of what I'm up to, confessing all in advance of the crime, you might say.

Gloucester is going to be big in this space because it's big with me . . . Gloucester people, Gloucester ways, the rough land and the Atlantic, the vessels and the fishing of now and then, the wharves, sailing, the weather, the uplands . . . sights, sounds, smells . . . past, present and future, yes, future.

The truth is that they're giving me all the sea room I need, to write what I damn please in. But I shall play it cool and keep her reefed down for the present. Let Buchwald, Plante and the rest take the world for their oyster; I'll have my hands full trying to figure out what some cynics claim is at the end of it.

Now I have strong feelings about Gloucester. It's been in my blood for about 300 years, which I suppose is long enough to sour a person's temper but sweeten his outlook. This town is the squarest and contrariest peg anyone ever broke his hammer on trying to pound into the round hole of conformity to anything.

Being de facto islanders, Gloucester people and Cape Anners generally are a skeptical breed. So to get to the windward of you, I must sail closehauled, tacking back and forth, and luffing as necessary.

If the helm seems to wander and the course is less than true, bear with me. This is a windward voyage of rediscovery to search out the sources of confidence and pride and sense of identity and direction, and good values that I believe we once had in Gloucester and which I fear we have mislaid, in company with the rest of America.

Have we forgotten our rugged history, our heroic and inspiring maritime tradition, or have we foolishly brushed it aside as if the hand of the past (the past to which we are all slaves or heirs, we cannot deny it) did not lay heavily on us today, as indeed it does?

We have defaulted to cynicism, know-nothingism and despair. We're letting the fast-buck artists and the homegrown carpetbaggers and the well-poisoners grab our real estate, mess up our neighborhoods, despoil our landscape and sell out our futures, that is, our children.

Ancient Rome would have regarded our public water system as a disgrace, and we dispose of our collective sewage as if we were animals, I mean in our midst. So hardened are we to existing in the presence of our own filth that the State, like a long-suffering parent, had literally to force us to stop burning our trash and breeding our rats in our bedroom.

But progress cannot be repressed forever. A new administration is about to take the field, and from the outside professional city manager on down, there will be some newcomers to join the Irish, English, Novies, Newfies, Portuguese, Italians, Finns, Jews, Swedes, Greeks, Lebanese, French and other out-of-towners who have kept old Gloucester on the map for 350 years. And thank God for them.

No, the once greatest fishing port in the universe is not going to fade out of the picture without struggle, not after all these years. I don't believe it. The open spaces and the marshes will not be erased from the land. Neither grass nor chaos will take hold in our streets.

Our taxes, though we deserve them and more for our sins of neglect, will not drive us out. Belief in the future will return. Plans will be laid. The water will at last be drinkable, and the waste disposed of as humans should. The harbor will be cleaned up, the waterfront restored, the schools made fit for the children and our young people given hope.

Imagine the prospect that one day, right here in Gloucester we will lift ourselves by our bootstraps, into the 20th century.

On this jolly note, and with no special insights or rights to tell my neighbors how to think or what to do, but only my particular view of things and some knack for putting it on paper, I shall hereby proceed in my own foolhardy fashion to preach cajole, entertain, reminisce, predict, pontificate, sentimentalize, castigate, jest and affront, according as the mood strikes me, but lay me low if I ever bore.

What will come of it all, I can't say. But this I know. . .the flame, be it ever so faint, is worth the candle.

So much for the first batch of pancakes, and have a thankful Thanksgiving.

November 20, 1967

Beating to
Windward

2. GOOD FOR YOU GUYS! —~~—

THE YEAR 1968, AS WE WERE LEARNING from the kids, was the pits. The Vietnam War was tearing both countries apart. It killed the New Frontier and its author and was holding Lyndon Johnson, his Great Society, the civil rights movement, and about everything and everybody else hostage. Martin Luther King and Robert Kennedy were murdered. The Democratic Convention in Chicago was an antidemocratic nightmare to rival the war. Language, at best, was inadequate to it all. But there were glimmers. Americans with moral as well as physical courage began standing up for themselves and each other, and the Supreme Court stood up for all of us.

As a combat foot soldier of '43-44, I was invulnerable to the hawks and could speak from experience in war. Might Vietnam have been brought to an earlier end, or never been embarked on, if we veterans who knew war and the results of war had shared those nightmares and fears for the future with those who knew them not?

PERSONALLY, I THINK YOUNG Howard Marston is a pretty courageous kid for resisting the draft. So are the boys who are submitting to it, taking their bitter medicine and preparing to fight, as the law of the land requires them to, in a war over which their country is so painfully divided.

The Rockport lad's answer to compulsory military service is to refuse to be a party to the destruction of the Vietnamese, to risk jail in his opposition to what he calls an illegal and immoral war.

The rest of the guys, on the other hand, feel that their personal opinions of the war and their moral scruples or reservations — to the extent that these considerations weigh upon them — fall away before their duty to serve their country and its leaders, right or wrong.

Are not the resister and the draftee the ones who are facing up to their dilemma most honestly, with the greater courage? One is prepared for prison and scorn, the other to inflict and risk destruction in a dubious cause.

In the middle are those caught in the toils, searching for some other means to avoid or to resolve the terrible dilemma with which we have burdened our youth. And have we the right to judge them, we cynics who oppose the war, as I do, and yet so dutifully pay the taxes that support it? Do any of us who are not subject to the call have the right to judge any of them who are?

Twice blessed as I am with daughters, I always wanted a

son too, but now I thank God I have none.

Howard Marston's father and mother have invoked their parental prerogative and forbidden their minor son to enter the army, thereby risking prosecution themselves for counseling resistance to the draft.

Can a minor who is of draftable but not legal age be jailed for placing the commands of his parents above those of his country? The father, particularly, has thus interjected himself into his son's decision and raised the question whether Howard Jr. is acting entirely of his own free will or out of submission to parental influence and orders. In either case, the boy's courage is undeniable

Obviously the Selective Service system would be unable to enforce the draft of minors if parents were allowed to reserve unrestricted right of jurisdiction over their offspring until the age of 21. It is the old irony: too young to vote, old enough to die — not likely to be resolved in a society run by the too old to die.

Perhaps the Marstons and their attorneys hope for a chance to battle it out along these lines, although no one has yet struck successfully at the roots of compulsory military service, however arbitrary or undemocratic or unfair it may be. No one is likely to so long as the nation is unable to find a more equitable way of raising an army or to outlaw war.

Generally the world does not seem to intrude on us in a raw and troublesome way here on this island called Cape Ann. Most of the rough issues of the day don't penetrate this far.

There is scarcely a Negro in Gloucester or Rockport or Essex or Manchester to disturb our complacence, so that civil rights and the challenges of Black Power remain academic matters. There is rather little extreme poverty, though a great many of our people (if we dare look around us) are just getting by.

But the one overriding issue, the one we can't escape, is the war and our impotence in the face of it. Here at the end of the world, as we like to fancy ourselves, there is no boundary, no amount of insulation, that can hold this world back, this world of death and mayhem that enters every home every night on the TV, that sinks itself into every one of us.

It's the boys age 20 to 26 who are taking the heat, the whole brunt of it. The rest of us can argue, hate, demonstrate and write Congress for and against. But these are the young bloods who, while all the shouting's going on, have to make up their minds somehow out of the depths of their inexperience whether to resist, to evade, or to follow.

They are getting damn little help from their bewildered and leaderless elders. From one day to the next, there is precious little we can do for them except to offer them sympathy in their (and our) dilemma, understanding in their ordeal, support in their decisions.

As for you, Howard Marston, I salute you and Jonathan Pope and Jannik von Rosenvinge and your fellow resisters for your courage, and Chairman Bertram Allen of your draft board for having the courage to commend your courage, and I salute all you other young men, all of you, for the courage it takes to be young men in America today.

January 2, 1968

3. I'M ON THE LINE FOR GENE ~~~

A NEWSPAPER COLUMNIST WHO wants to gain and retain the confidence of his readers — and this has nothing to do with whether they agree with him or not — should probably avoid entangling alliances.

If he would present a strongly independent point of view, as this column has attempted to on occasion, he ought to be a sort of involved isolationist — certainly not an international one — holding himself apart from the passing scene, yet deeply concerned about it. But if a time arrives when he feels he must commit himself to cause or individual, as partisan or advocate, he owes it to his readers and to his publisher to do it publicly.

This columnist regards the opportunity to occupy this space twice a week, without the slightest hint of interference from his newspaper, as a rare privilege and a public trust.

Conscience, moral outrage, intellectual revulsion, heartsickness over the war persuaded me to accept the chairmanship of the Cape Ann McCarthy for President Committee, to commit myself, to add my mite to what I fervently hope is a growing movement for a sane foreign policy.

In a fearfully short while, during which American manpower in Vietnam has increased 30-fold and we have dropped more explosives on that scarred scrap of earth than on all of Europe during World War II, the Administration's policy has been reduced from bravado to bewilderment to bankruptcy.

The Cong is everywhere and gaining strength by the hour. Our Saigon puppets are on the verge of evaporation. We have scorched the blood and land of Vietnam with more devastation from the air alone than descended with the two atomic bombs on Japan.

We have suffered dreadful casualties, and avenged them against a population. We have been assured again and again that we are winning, and we are losing, for all of Asia will go against us at the rate we're making friends, and there are two billion souls in the Far East and the Soviet Union.

But what is past is over and done. Where do we go now? Do we keep escalating? Can we? And if so where, how, against whom? Where does escalation lead, if they can do it just as well or better?

Do we pull back to the enclave? Presently we have no choice. And from the enclave, where? What will happen to the fortress theory at Khe Sanh?

Do we pull out? Impossible, not just like that. Do we negotiate? We must.

We must halt the bombing, admit that we've taken our licks, negotiate a strategic disengagement, recognize the National Liberation Front, concede the necessity of a coalition government while there is a chance of it, gradually turn Vietnam back to the Vietnamese and reassess the entire basis of our Asian foreign policy.

All this before it's too late and we're going too fast to follow the twists in the road ahead, the hairpin turns of reality in a world we may yet be able to lead but can never control.

As I see it, this is the essence of Senator McCarthy's philosophy in his campaign for the Democratic nomination, a practical political alternative to our present foreign policy.

This is the great service he is rendering his countrymen and in fact the democratic process. He is offering Americans of all persuasions who want to end the war — as honorably as possible, I think — the chance to express themselves at the polls, to vote on the issue in the time-honored way. No other announced candidate has the political courage.

The *Gloucester Times* has commended the Senator editorially for his public service but suggests that he is not a great persuader, that he does not convey a sense of urgency, that he is "fuzzy," that perhaps he is half dove and half hawk, that "hybrids don't get elected."

Well, I say the same about this *Times* editorial of January 29, and I might add that the future of the nation and the world may depend upon the election of just such a hybrid, one who is neither propagandist nor demagogue and just fuzzy enough to recognize that we do not live on a planet governed by absolutes, that neither the dove nor the hawk is equipped to cope, alone, with the real enemies — power, hunger, violence, greed, fear and hate.

All around me I see the shambles, not of the Great Society, but of the dream of the New Frontier, which was of hope for our future, of faith in our land and people, of pride in ourselves.

I see on the screen our boys, their boys, their women, their children, about to die, dying, maimed, dead — a war more horrible than any I knew at first-hand a quarter of a century ago.

I see the face of Vietnam. I hear the cry of humanity. We are doing great wrong. This is why I commit myself to the cause of Senator Eugene McCarthy.

February 16, 1968

4. IS DISSENT GETTING RESPECTABLE? ~⚋~

IT SEEMS LIKE A LONG, LONG TIME ago that this column was foolhardy enough to call young Howard Marston of Rockport a pretty courageous kid for resisting the draft. And for good measure tossed a similar salute to Jon Pope and Nik von Rosenvinge.

And likewise to all the young men, draftees and resisters, for the courage it takes to be young men in America today. And was it not echoing what most everybody feels, that the overriding issue of the day, the ever present nightmare that we cannot escape from, is the war and our impotence in the face of it?

That was the 12th of January, and I guess I figured I was trotting out to left field without a glove

But the barrage never came. More expressions of support than condemnation were heard, though there was scattered flak, and it really began to seem just possible that the day was dawning when an ordinary person could raise some questions about the war and the drafting and the killing of legions of our boys and unnumbered thousands of our presumed enemies and the sacredness of the assumptions that propped up this madness, and do it without being castigated as a commie, dupe, bleeding heart, idiot, coward, traitor, nigger-lover, nonsupporter of our boys, pal of Ho or Subversive Serf in the Realm of King Lyndon.

Since then, the draft resisters, their supporters, advocates and sympathizers have become an almost familiar fixture in the landscape of protest.

Taking heart, this column a few weeks later issued a David's challenge to the Goliath of Gloucester tradition that it is good educational practice to force our high school boys into uniforms, snap them around the drill field and gym floor — yes, like toy soldiers — and drag them by the pink lobes of their ears through a canned course in how to kill, kill, kill.

Well, supposed I, you've put the old foot in it now.

But instead of fallout, what happened? The boys started passing around petitions respectfully suggesting that ROTC be made elective. Superintendent Stan Thompson supported the idea of change, and so did five of the seven members of the School Committee.

It remains only for the majority to vote their expressed convictions and take the compulsion out of this pocket of militarism in our midst that so loosely permits adolescents to slouch around the streets idly pointing rifles at the public.

And then of course there was the slow build-up of Senator Eugene McCarthy's campaign that attracted the disdain of editorial writers and some columnists and the commitment of this one in particular, his lightning rod-like evocation of public opinion in New Hampshire and of the energy and idealism of youth everywhere, and as a consequence the decision of Senator Bobby Kennedy to come clean himself, if not exactly for Gene.

The Texas dam that has been holding back the rising waters of dissent is crumbling, cracking, making very scary noises, and it is the most hopeful thing that has happened since the election of Jack Kennedy.

Dissent is once again getting to be respectable. Debate that means something is returning. It has to be fertilized. Only out of the free soil of debate does a democracy grow rational policy and careful action.

It will be a great day when we can reason together, as the President has not thought fit to do for so long, and cast aside the tired-out, hackneyed slogans of hawk and dove, free world, communist menace, consensus, black power overkill, backlash and all the rest, and do our own thinking, each of us, for a change.

Do we dare hope that the shock waves of questioning, of dissent, of debate will pick up enough height and power to cause King Lyndon and the Knights of the Pentagon to reconsider whether it is really necessary, politically or otherwise, to inflict upon the upland watershed of Cape Ann and any where else the utterly useless and discredited fiasco known as the Sentinel Missile System?

And can we dream, at least, that the exploding debate within the Democratic Party, which seems always ready to renew its life this way, may encourage the Republicans to reenter the two-party system and Governor Rockefeller to extend the borders of his publicly expressed concern with the nation's fate and future rather beyond the collection of garbage in her largest city?

Time has a way of telling. And America has a way of surviving as long as people keep doing their own thinking, making dissent respectable.

March 18, 1968

5. Challenge to the Cape Ann clergy —⁓—

A MONTH AGO THERE WAS A PASS-ing, almost unnoticed dialogue in this newspaper between two Lanesville pastors over the application today of Christ's injunction: "Render therefore unto Caesar the things which are Caesar's; and unto God the things which are God's."

Discussing the avenues of action open to a young man facing the draft, the Rev. Harvey L. Pierce of the Orthodox Congregational Church had concluded: "Obedience to God is the clearest expression of confidence in Him. Obedience to our government shows confidence in it. If the spirit of rebellion continues to grow against it then we shall eventually be weakened to the point where our enemies can destroy us.

"Certainly our enemies do not profess to be Christian at all. For the conscientious person and

Christian, then, obedience is the way to serve God and country."

Pierce's position was challenged by the Rev. Thomas B. Chittick of St. Paul Lutheran Church, who thought its implications were "close to the policy used by many German church leaders during Hitler's rise to power who so championed obedience to civil authority that they 'baptized' that beast — the Nazi reign of terror."

Chittick was referring to the attack in the Book of Revelation on civil authority as a "beast mouthing bombast and blasphemy." He continued: "So, regarding Vietnam protesters and the question of the draft, I may or may not agree with their thinking and methods, but I will die for their right to say what they believe not only because it is, fortunately, a part of the great American experiment in democ-

racy, but because the testimony of Scripture warns us against thinking that we can so cavalierly assume God's sanction rests with a particular policy, government or tradition."

Now here, to this agnostic, is a most significant exchange. One preacher says, in effect, "Ours is not to reason why; ours is but to do or die." And that is what our civil authority is telling us today — and our young men.

The man on the other side of the street seems to be summoning up the words of Thomas Jefferson: "Indeed, I tremble for my country when I reflect that God is just."

That these very different interpretations of the nature and obligations of American citizenship should revolve around the stand taken by the draft resisters is quite to the point. Most of those of us who are over 21 have some recourse to the ballot box in the determination of our national policy, pitifully limited as that may be.

But the only positive form of self-expression open to the boy who is old enough to have his guts blown out in Vietnam but too young to enter the polling booth is resistance. The principle of conscientious objection, as Bernard Shaw observed, is a feeble ruse which by its very acceptance indicts the whole machinery.

Here on Cape Ann we have two traditions in this tremendously important area of the self-determination of the individual. On the one hand there is the ancient way of the fisherman, who for 350 years has been going down to the sea to bring back the bounty which the Lord put there, and which for 350 years has enriched the men who owned the vessels and the gear, the shoreside facilities and the means of distribution and sale, in short the capital.

This is the tradition of the fisherman. You do your job, you risk all or you lose it, you make your owner's profit even if the trip's a broker, and you don't question the system for a mo-

ment, not for 350 years, that has kept you poor all your life while the Old Man built his great house on the hill.

Yet within that system, where it all comes out of the hold, playing the rules of the Old Man's game, you fight with incredible courage and ingenuity the powers of the sea and the elements and the swing of fortune, and you die or fade out in the struggle of it. But you don't question the system or its premises, whether it is right or just, economically, morally or any other way for you or your progeny, any more than your fathers and your forefathers questioned.

This is one tradition, but there is another, of John Wise, the Ipswich minister, who in 1687 defied the kingly power of the Crown's governor of Massachusetts Bay in one of the earliest acts of civil disobedience in the New World which, reinforced by his ringing statement of liberty thirty years later, helped to lay the groundwork for the American Revolution.

And the tradition of John Murray, founder of Universalism in America, persecuted pastor of the First Universalist Church in Gloucester, whose re-

fusal, with his flock, to pay taxes to the established church was one of the first test cases upholding the separation of church and state.

So we have these traditions on Cape Ann of quiet, stolid, unquestioning, courageous acceptance of things as they are and always have been, the wisdom of the seafarer — and the tradition of dissent, of freethinking, the way of the gnawing conscience, of the pioneer of the spirit.

What do the clergy of Cape Ann, our religious and moral leaders, have to say about the two terrible crises of our time, the war in Vietnam and racism in America? What does the Cape Ann Council of Churches have to say to us, passing through the valley of the shadow of death?

March 22, 1968

6. HOW SOME CHURCH PEOPLE TOOK IT ⁓

THE SUBJECT OF THIS CONCLUDING interfaith panel of the Council of Churches was "The Church Faces Social Issues." It was ten days before Easter, the lily-white Easter of Cape Ann. Having "challenged" the clergy, I was there as an invited observer.

They had shown a film, there in the basement of the First Baptist Church, which attempted to jog people into getting involved. It opened with the murder of Kitty Genovese in Manhattan in front of 38 uninvolved witnesses. Then there were comments by the panel, such as Mrs. Bernard Cohen's impatient indictment of Gloucester's refusal to recognize the extent of drug use here among young people, and the crying need for sex education.

We here in the churches have got to face up to this terrible problem of our noninvolve-ment, said the Rev. Bill Stayton of the Baptist Church, the chairman. And with rising voice, he exhorted: "The Massachusetts Council of Churches has just voted to call on every church in the state to place absolute top priority in its program of education and discussion and action on the two great issues of our time — the crisis in our inner cities, our ghettos, and the morality of the war in Vietnam."

At this precise moment a man hurried forward from the rear of the room and whispered to Mr. Stayton. There was a pause, and the clergyman said these words into the microphone: "Martin Luther King Jr. has been assassinated."

There was a momentary quiet, a few gasps, and a buzz of low talk. It was a total shock to most of us, but not all.

A few had heard the news just before arriving for the meeting. No one, until this moment, had bothered to notify the moderator of the discussion, subject "The Detached Churchmen."

"This could be awful," whispered a woman near me. "At least he controlled 'em."

Bill Stayton resumed then. Study after study, declared this mild man with all the emphasis at his command, has found that church people are more prejudiced racially and religiously than non-church people. What does this mean to us?

The trouble is, said a man in the audience, that what the Negro wants is money, and that's all he wants, money, and that's too much, he wants too much, where is it going to come from?

That's not what he wants, countered Father John Maguire of Sacred Heart Church angrily. He wants to be treated like a human being.

Look, said the man in the audience, it's too bad about this man King, but I tell you he knew what he was doing, he knew before he ever started his march on Washington it would end in a riot. This King threatened us that if they didn't get what they wanted, everything, there would be violence.

Let 'em go to work, said another woman near me in a low voice.

Before he came to Lanesville, Father Maguire commented, he tried to persuade the white members of his parish of 15,000 in West Roxbury to invite Negroes into their homes for visits. One family volunteered.

Recently in Gloucester, Mrs. Cohen observed, a Negro family attempted to rent or buy a house in the city proper and was refused at every turn. Finally they found a place on the outskirts.

What about the legal liabilities of getting involved when you see some kind of a crime, asked another man, especially if it's someone you don't even know?

A young woman got to her feet. She had been talking to a civil rights leader and told him of her concern about her children and how they would react to Negroes after being brought up and educated in a community where there are none. The trouble is, she said she told him, that we have no problem in Gloucester, because there are no Negroes here.

Did you ever stop to think, he replied, that perhaps that might be your problem in Gloucester?

No eulogy to the assassinated moral leader of all America, black and white, was offered during the meeting. But a minute of silence at the close.

Afterwards, as coffee and cakes were being served, people stood about, and some may have talked of Dr. King for all I know.

One clergyman had tried to have a Vietnam Sunday on Cape Ann, when the preachers would agree to say something, anything, pro or con, about the moral issues of the war. His brethren could not agree on it.

Another minister shook his head sadly: "The churches here are reflection of the community."

I am so shocked and stunned this morning over what is happening in America that this report, incomplete to be sure, is all I can bring myself to say right now about Martin Luther King.

April 5, 1968

7. THE BELL TOLLS IN A DISTANT PLACE

THE WHISTLER SIGHS IN ON THE lightest of southerly airs. Shimmering reflections of the waxing moon palpitate the still waters of the cove. With placid whishes the wavelets wane on the beach below the open window. The breakwater fog bell tolls on and on and on.

Yet the night is clear, clear to Boston. So why does the bell toll? For whom? What requiem is this, on this distant Eastern Point, in this distant place called Cape Ann where the endless sea meets the close shore, this endless night?

Out of these sounds of his boyhood here, out of the emptiness of his prime, T.S. Eliot wrote of the bell buoy tolling on the ground swell, a time older
Than time counted by anxious worried women
Lying awake, calculating the future,

Trying to unweave, unwind, unravel
And piece together the past and the future,
Between midnight and dawn, when the past is all deception,
The future futureless . . .

Downstairs on the television they are bringing Bobby's body up the steps into

Tom Eliot on the porch at Eastern Point, 1897

St. Patrick's Cathedral.

Which is the reality? The serenity of the Gloucester night, its warmth, its soothing sounds, the wafted sweetness of the honeysuckle, and through it all the tolling of the bell, inexorable, automatic, hollow clang?

Or the click of the switch, the squeeze on the trigger? Is that where the action is, behind the tube, among the odors of stale food in the kitchen of the Ambassador Hotel?

Is the reality a strange and nightmarish underground film? Is it a dreadful Celtic seaside tragedy of Synge? Is it the Man from Uncle? Is it always sock-it-to-me time?

Is what is happening really the reality, the straight stuff, no script, what you wake up to in the morning out of one of those despairing dreams that invade the mind just at the end of sleep, half awake, to know that you are still alive and it is the beginning of one more day nearer the end?

Yes, this is what it is. It is the real thing, all of it: From the pool of blood on the hotel kitchen floor, to the quietness of the tuned-out night in this old back-watered fish port, to the aberrant waves in the sick brain of a young Jordanian vomited up to posterity by the volcanic hatred of Arab and Jew, from sweet Bonnie's love for her simple Clyde to a yelping family game of touch football to ten thousand tons of napalm.

Is Eliot right then? Is the past all deception, the future futureless?

No, I won't believe it, not because I deny it but because as a spawn of the human race I can't bear to accept it.

Our world has stunk with murder in thought and deed since the first man-ape found that he could grasp a rock and bash his brother's skull in.

Last week our casualties were the highest in the war. And you can work your bloody way back through the retrogress of history, scuffing up the dust of millions upon millions of your brethren exterminated by our ancestry like insects.

But I will not believe that the poet is right.

I look in the mirror and I see the violence in myself. I look at you and I see it in you. You and I are animals.

But we know we are animals, and that is what sets us apart from the rest of the animal kingdom. That and the sophistication of our violence.

Consequently, when we murder by thought and deed there is at least the possibility that we may feel remorse for ourselves and even for each other, if not for our victims.

Upon this unique capacity to suffer guilt — I say guilt, not self-hate — depends the continued existence of the human animal. We have no other that can save us, and for the sake of no other, unhappily, are we worth saving.

June 7, 1968

8. THAT BIG BLACK TRUCK KEEPS COMING ⎯ᴍ⎯

SOMETIMES THINGS SEEM TO CATCH up with you and just overwhelm you. That's the way I feel now. Or at least a big part of me does.

The way events are bearing down on us brings to mind something that happened when I was about five, living not far from where the Kennedy boys started out.

Anyway I think it happened. Every few years it comes back to me, a recurrent thing that I somehow relive with all the terror I felt 40 years ago.

I was crossing a street above Brookline Village, a block from our house, when out of nowhere a truck bore down on me — one of those old black high-centered behemoths, maybe a Mack.

There was only time to throw myself down in the street, and the truck passed right over me. In my mind's eye I can see the dark chassis a few inches above my face, the spinning wheels on either side. And then it was gone, rattling down the hill.

It didn't touch me.

This must have happened, because the event is so vivid and has been relived so often. It might have been a dream that afflicted me all those years ago, but I don't think so. It really doesn't make any difference. It's as vivid either way, so the effect is the same.

I guess plenty of people have had or thought they had the same crazy kind of experience in their childhood that haunts them just often enough to keep alive the reality of it, yet mixing the mental image and the event into an indistinguishable nightmare.

It's the way I feel now, like I was lying in the street and the truck was over me. Yes I know. The truck will pass, and everything will be all right again. War, bombs, defoliation, jellied gasoline, riots, Resurrection City, assassination, half-starving American kids, pot, student civil war, cigarette ads that use murder and sex to sell cancer and heart disease to a generation of 12-year-olds . . . and everything will be all right.

Like hell it will.

Four months ago a neighbor got the news that her nephew had been killed in Vietnam. Now her son has received his orders to ship out.

I say like hell everything will be all right.

Too many people that I know are tuning out, not just on the signals from over the horizon but on what's screaming to be heard in the front yard and in the parlor and under the bed and in it, here in this idyllic retreat from the madness of mankind known as Cape Ann.

Don't we have to start somewhere to do something to bring some sanity back into our lives?

If one percent of the energy that is being spent in mourning Senator Kennedy and panicking over the state of the nation were directed into the same kind of concern and compassion that he felt for his fellow man, we would be back on the right track.

A few years ago I worked for a metropolitan newspaper in New England, *The Providence Journal*, that was very liberal about civil rights and the problems of the black man. They hired a black reporter and assigned him to do a series of articles exposing the conditions of his race.

In the paper's home city, where they had an abominable ghetto? Not on your life. They sent him down where the cotton grows so that none of the local slum lords would suffer bruised consciences.

So I say that if you and I are looking for somewhere to turn, if we feel as if that nightmare truck of mine is bearing down on us — well, maybe it is, and maybe the Judgment Day is at hand.

But in the meanwhile we can go down fighting. We can stop lying to ourselves about the kind of world we're living in, right here on Cape Ann, about the lies we're living and the lives we're wasting.

If we could look to ourselves for some of Bobby Kennedy's sense of outrage and his particular feeling for youth and put it to work against the inequities, the apathy, the violence, the self-delusion and despair which I am afraid characterize too many aspects of life here, we would be doing something to push back the madness that seems to be bearing down on America like that black truck of my subconscious.

We've got to begin somewhere, or we're going to be cannibalized by the humans who don't even know they're animals.

June 10, 1968

9. WARREN COURT MAY HAVE SAVED DEMOCRACY —ⁿⁿ—

CHIEF JUSTICE EARL WARREN's retirement from the Supreme Court before the election to insure the succession of another liberal will tax what little self-control his enemies have left.

The attacks of the extreme right wing on the highest tribunal and their wolf pack demands for the impeachment of the distinguished American who presides over it have been paranoid in the violence of their hatred.

But posterity, that supreme judge, will decide, I think, that the 15 years of the Warren era have been perhaps the most significant to the preservation of our constitutional principles and probably the most judicially courageous in the history of this branch of the government,

The philosophical momentum of the majority seems likely to prevail for the foresee-able future, regardless of turns in the political road.

It has been and is a libertarian Court, and at the same time, curiously, a conservative one. The great decisions, striking through the irrelevance and hysteria of these tormented and chaotic years, have time and again scored in the heart of the American conscience.

Landmarks all, but radical only to the extent that they have stripped away the bewilderment and preoccupation, the frustration and fear and hate, and forced us to look at ourselves in the national mirror, to compare the image with the reality, to ask what happened to the American Purpose.

What has the Warren Court accomplished?

In 1954 it decided that the Constitution forbids racial segregation in our public schools, and so broke a 90-year moratorium on justice for black Americans and created the civil rights movement.

It concluded in 1962 that religious observance in public schools is inconsistent with the founding principle of separation, conceived so bitterly out of some of history's hardest lessons — the principle of noninterference between church and state embodied in the First Amendment.

In 1964 it began the process of reshuffling the stacked political deck when it ordered that Congressional and state legislative districts be redrawn to provide each citizen equal representation, wherever he lives.

By redressing the balance of geographical power and giving the urban voter, especially, his due, this decision may prove to have fashioned the single most potent political instrument for dealing democratically and effectively with the crisis in the cities.

And two years ago the Warren Court spelled out the constitutional rights of persons accused of crime (note "accused," not criminals yet) to maintain silence under questioning and to be represented by a lawyer.

These far-reaching affirmations of the civil rights and liberties of Americans, and the many others that reflect the application of the Court's philosophy to everything from housing to loyalty, have come under the most unrestrained assaults by extremists who view the Supreme Court as a sort of Pandora's Box, as if the problems it has been grappling with existed only in the imaginations of nine men who have proceeded to release them under the guise of decisions, like a plague, on the fair and otherwise untroubled face of the land.

Less naive citizens have found much in these decisions that upsets them, particularly those who have to deal with them or implement them, like school administrators, politicians, law enforcement officials,

and all of us, really, because the Court has been making it impossible for America to turn away from its inner reality.

So it strikes me that the Warren bench has been a great conservative force in the nation during at least half of a period of almost continual crisis that goes back to the Depression.

Franklin D. Roosevelt attempted 35 years ago to bend another Supreme Court to his will and failed, fortunately, and it is ironic that a good many of those who hated him during the New Deal as a radical and "traitor" to privilege concede now that he was a conservative who saw the necessity of drastic treatment for the salvation of the system.

The Cold War and irrational fear of communism, the old witch hunt, the pressures for conformity, the widening inequalities, the crises of racism, of poverty, of the cities, and of the expression of frustration and widespread mental illness in violent forms — these underlie the monumental issues that have pressed themselves on the highest court.

It has reacted conservatively. It has said: The strength and vigor of this nation and its

institutions are rooted absolutely in the freedom of the individual and in the body of law and precedent that proclaims and protects that freedom. Whatever else we gain, if we lose that we lose all.

And so the Court has gone back over and over again to first principles, to the national conscience and purpose, to reaffirm and extend the protection of the Constitution and Bill of Rights as it is charged to interpret them — like the good doctor prescribing for his patient, no matter how much it hurts.

Perhaps because we have suffered from our weakest political leadership since 1931 during most of these years of painful crisis that Earl Warren has been presiding, the major struggles within the American conscience — except for the Vietnam War — have been worked out behind those massive pillars, quite possibly to our salvation as a democracy.

For not shrinking from these times of national soul-searching, we can take pride in our Chief Justice and his associates.

June 24, 1968

When antiwar Senator Eugene McCarthy swept the New Hampshire Democratic primary in 1968, President Johnson saw the handwriting, withdrew from reelection, and gave the nod to Vice President Hubert Humphrey, who was steamrolled through the unspeakable Democratic convention in August by Chicago Mayor Daley's machine, only to be defeated by Richard Nixon's comeback in November, beginning fifteen years of Republicanism. I followed the Chicago debacle on television and forced myself to write a daily column. Here are two.

10. FRUSTRATION AND HATE: NO ONE IS IMMUNE —⁓—

IT'S SO QUIET AND PEACEFUL HERE on Cape Ann, surrounded by the sea, the air crisp with the waning summer, that Chicago really seems unbelievable. You felt somewhat the same way after Robert Kennedy's assassination.

But Chicago — and Miami Beach — happened, all right. They are real. They are America, and we are America. The conventions this month are reflections of you and me, as if the picture tube were a mirror.

The Republican affair, its well-oiled and bland and affluent dullness, and the inevitability of its outcome, reflected that side of Americans that turns away from reality by refusing to recognize the explosiveness of our national crisis.

In Chicago, that teeming non-city in the wrenched heart of the United States, it all came out as it is yesterday. Not just the

Democratic Party but the whole nation displayed its wounds, and the hurt could not be hidden.

The delegates agonized over Vietnam, but in the end 60 percent of them couldn't summon the courage to call their party and President and themselves wrong.

Black America was squeezed out once again from another racist convention. Integrated southern delegations were barred from the doors by liberal northern delegations, and tokenism ruled.

Where were Ralph Abernathy and his poor people, the darlings of the Democrats and so evident at Miami Beach? The poor, like the blacks, are on their own.

As for the platform on which the party proposes to lead us to better days over the next four years, only the Vietnam

plank was debated, and the rest of it wasn't even read aloud. Thus did the bosses show their contempt for delegates and public alike.

And what did the Democrats have to offer the young people whose lives are being thrown away in Vietnam and who had come to Chicago, with such futility, to protest?

The clubs, the mace, the tear gas, the brutality of Daley's storm troopers, and the bayonets of Johnson's National Guard.

Blood in the lobby of the Hilton. A presidential nominee sent to the showers in his lofty suite by the fumes of the battlefield below, with genuine tears for once.

No, the kids shouldn't have lobbed pop bottles and stones at the cops. But you saw the way Daley preserves law and order. Judge for yourself, and if you are old enough, picture the newsreels of the nineteen thirties. Prague speaks for itself, as Bobby's giant bodyguard Roosevelt Grier suggested.

Inside the Amphitheater the Democrats disemboweled themselves for the color cameras. You saw Boss Daley, his delegation of minions pressed to his cold bosom by a cordon of plainclothesmen, passing his throat-slitting signals to the podium, instructing whose mike was to be cut off.

Daley and Criswell executed the putsch of Chicago. But Lyndon B. Johnson engineered it. The President could have had the convention anywhere he wanted, but he chose Chicago for reasons that have become increasingly visible to the TV viewer this week.

Is the press being trampled on — to use an old-fashioned expression — at Chicago? Again, judge for yourself. You saw Dan Rather punched and knocked to the floor, Mike Wallace punched and arrested, the clearly tightening censorship of TV by restriction of movement, reporters and cameramen singled out by cops in the streets and beaten to the asphalt.

These unbelievable events, these awful widening gulfs among Americans are being acted out in Chicago as if it were a stage. All the inequalities and the conflicting interests and injustices and the harvest that we reap from our war are stalking that stage. The frustration and hate they produce breed greater divisions and even more violent reactions.

None of us is immune. Did you see Bill Buckley on Channel 7? He was beside himself with rage at the needling of Gore Vidal and shouted: "If you don't shut up, I'll punch you in the goddamn face!"

And I reflect today on how I reacted yesterday to these proceedings by writing that "I'd like to go out and sock a pol, any pol, of either party,"

This hardly represents a fruitful approach to our problems, does it? Yet there are few of us, man or woman I think, who can honestly deny to ourselves that this violence born of frustration does not lurk somewhere within us.

Senator Eugene McCarthy, whom I have publicly supported for the past several months, didn't make it. And the things he stood for failed also to carry the day, although they came much closer to realization than his candidacy, in the Vietnam debate. Still, but for him there perhaps would have been no debate at all.

So it will be Humphrey and Nixon.

But somehow I don't believe that what McCarthy and the Kennedys and McGovern and Rockefeller and Lindsay, and most of all the coming generation, have turned on can so easily be shut off as Miami Beach and Chicago might lead you to think.

August 29, 1968

11. THE CANDIDATE OF CHAOS

THE EARTH TREMBLED, THE SEAS roared, the heavens flashed and the great Democratic mountain labored . . . and brought forth Hubert.

Smooth and jowled, glib, tearful, platitudinous as a southern Baptist preacher ... the choice of his party is the magician of the platform, ever eager to demonstrate that the mouth is quicker than the mind.

Would you buy a used car from this man?

The Battle of the Conventions is over. The body count is just beginning, but television has probably already determined the outcome in November, as it tipped the balance in 1960 from Richard Nixon to John Kennedy.

Images in these times have a way of turning into traps. In eight years Nixon appears to have succeeded in squirming at least part way out of his old image, and he conveys the impression now that some of his more positive qualities are on the ascendancy.

In any case, that is his new image.

Beyond this, he gained the Republican nomination by submitting to the public test, and he dominated the convention that chose him in the course of a superficially effective show of party unity.

Humphrey, on the other hand, has been moving in the opposite direction. He was at the peak of his popularity as a senator who worked long and hard and courageously for progressive measures and reforms from civil rights and health insurance in the domestic area to the nuclear test ban in the foreign.

I knew him slightly 21 years ago when he was the brash and brassy young Mayor of Minneapolis and I was a cub police reporter on the *Minneapolis Tribune*. I liked him.

What a worker! I was on the night shift at police headquarters in the basement of City Hall and fairly frequently, shortly before I was knocking off at two in the morning, His Honor would drop in for a cup of coffee with us at the sergeant's desk.

Humphrey had started work at around eight that morning and was just finishing an 18-hour day. He would shoot the bull with the cops and me for a few minutes, and we would talk some politics, and then his official chauffeur would drive him home.

All I recall from these encounters is a remark he dropped to me one night.

"You know, Joe," said he, "I have a political axiom that has served me well, and I expect to continue to live by it." Then, with a twinkle in his eye, the future presidential nominee rasped:

"Never get in a pissing contest with a skunk." *

Who knows what has happened to the Humphrey of the forties and the fifties? But he climbed to the top through the Old Politics, and the higher he rose, the more he compromised by making the right deals with the power brokers and pressure groups.

Today, he is the absolute captive of his image. Somewhere along the line his best qualities — his imagination, his engaging courage, his true zest, his realistic small-town optimism, above all his identification with common folk — have gone by the board. And his worst have come to control him and rule his personality.

Today Hubert Humphrey is the devoted handmaiden of Lyndon Johnson, and he has made a mockery of political loyalty.

Fifteen years ago he would have cried out against the awful events in Chicago and set the nation on its ear with his anger. And it is hard for me to imagine that in the Senate he would not have thrown the full force of his fury against this war.

Today, his words clang with emptiness. His principles are encrusted with the fat of political expediency. His humanity has given way to ambition. His imagination has taken refuge in self-delusion. His courage has deserted him in the final confrontation with men stronger than he.

Hubert Humphrey today is a hollow man. The compromises have been too much for him. He has dissipated his strength, and now only his weakness remains. He is lackey to every conflicting force in his party, their serf, from Johnson to Daley, from Maddox to Meany. He is the bitter fruit of chaos.

It was all there in his acceptance speech last night, the rankest sham and the hollowest hypocrisy of the Battle of the Conventions.

Outside, the skulls cracked and the blood flowed. Inside, the Daleys and the Connollys clapped and beamed like the proud parents of a high school valedictorian.

Hubert Horatio Humphrey talked and he talked, but he had nothing to say any more to anybody.

August 30, 1968

---

* "pissing" was too much for my friend, the late Bill Cahill, who edited this particular piece and left a blank. Times and the *Times* have changed.

12. THIS WAS NO TURNED-ON TRIP 〜

IT WAS A ROUND-TRIP TICKET TO the moon in Apollo II after all, much to nobody's surprise. So successful has the space program been that it leaves you in a daze; what would have been mind-shattering ten years ago is almost, but not quite, ho-hum today.

Except, that it *is* mind exploding. The guys dance in the moon dust, leave an olive branch behind, deliver in-flight lectures to the rest of mankind on the meaning of it all, and back home again are goggled at by the President of the United States in their glass incubator like precious but premature triplets.

Was there ever such a trip on LSD? Can psychedelics compare with the kind of ride you get in LEM? The drug hop loses his grip, bursts the synapses of his brain and sells what separates him from animals into narcotic slavery.

Millions of down-to-earth people watched Armstrong and Aldrin step onto the front porch of the universe, live and alive, Sunday night and walked forth with them. That was a trip to expand the mind and transport the soul, if there be such a thing.

But the tricks drugs play on that good gray matter the users abuse are sordid fakes alongside the stuff men are doing and dreaming of in the cool, unpolluted recesses of the human cerebrum.

Mind-shattering in the wave-after-wave of its implications, this latest Apollo mission is but as simple and as neat and as logical in the accomplishment as a pyramid.

Inspect the green side of a dollar bill and you will see the Great Seal depicting a pyramid. In place of its incompleted apex gazes forth the unblinking eye of God, without whose agency no work of man is ever done.

Lest we forget, Apollo was god of the sun, the source of all energy, and hence life, in this molecule in the ocean of the universe we call the solar system.

Should we presume to approach the sun god too boldly, so mythology warns, he will melt the wax that secures our wings, as he did those of the foolish Icarus, and we will plunge into the sea, without benefit of parachute.

But what a pyramid, all the same! Built out of the sum of human knowledge and achievement, and possibly wisdom — each piece resting nigh perfectly upon its predecessors.

What a fabric of inspiration and selection it represents! Archimedes, Hippocrates, Euclid, Galen, Copernicus, Galileo, Magellan, Harvey, Newton,

Descartes, Lavoisier, Wright, Edison, Einstein, Goddard of Worcester, Hammond of Gloucester, Glenn, Kraft, Joe Doaks.

It was as if all of humanity, in one vast, convulsive lurch had concentrated everything it had learned in twenty-five thousand years in order to eject three of its fledglings from the terrestrial nest into space.

And what of those three? Are they a new race, something more than earthlings? Have they lived to see the upper Orpheus in triumph? What are they to us, these quick, bright, so very likable, so very American, young men? I don't think we know yet whether they are truly a new breed or merely a new twist in a very old one, but their courage and their coolness and intelligence and humanity and all the circumstances of their feat surely add up to a new kind of hero.

There will always be a place for the old-fashioned loner as long as our highly organized society allows eccentrics like Hilary, Cousteau, Centennial Johnson and Howard Blackburn and Francis Chichester to pit themselves against themselves and the elements in lonely, self-reliant combat.

Armstrong, Aldrin and Collins, on the other hand, are organization men and, more than that, essentially social men. They were launched from a pyramid built painstakingly out of the ability of thousands upon thousands to create, to take responsibility and to cooperate in a fashion unprecedented in the history of technology.

Yet this whole pyramid was as strong as the weakest stone or piece of mortar in it. The world has probably known of no human endeavor to compare with the Apollo program since the invasion of Normandy. But in this case, one wrong button pressed, and all could have been lost.

Faith, then, strikes me as the outstanding quality common to all our astronauts. Transcendent faith in themselves and in each other; absolute, almost religious if you will, faith in all that thrust them out there, kept them there, and brought them back — from Sir Isaac Newton's First Law of Motion to the skill of an anonymous and unsung technician in Kalamazoo with a soldering iron.

That men in this shattering world today, on this torn earth, can find this faith and parlay it into a round trip voyage to the moon — this for me is the mind-restoring meaning of Apollo II.

July 25, 1969

13. IT RAINS BUT OUR THROATS ARE DRY ⁓⁓

WILL THE RAINS NEVER CEASE? The summer squash rots on the vine, the tomatoes won't ripen, doors won't shut, windows won't open, and this poor crag of rock we live on sprouts with the green of the tropics. And still it rains, and fogs, and drips and drenches.

What crazy contrasts. A few summers ago we were a desert and Public Works told us to dump bricks in the water closet. Last February we lived in the Arctic: no power, no phone, no bread, ten-foot drifts, ice ruts to your hubcaps and the Army to the rescue.

What crazy contrasts, even for New England. And the peaks and valleys seem to get higher and deeper, as if these extremes of climate were merely reflecting an even greater starkness in our world where the opposites grow more dramatic, more abrupt, harsher by the day —

like the dead cold black shadows cast by the rocks and craters of the moon, a step from the sun's unremitting heat.

My Calvinist background makes me suspicious of too much of a good thing, for there is something decadent, sickly sweet, about such lushness on our usually barren cape. It smacks of rot.

I am reminded of the plain that spread out before us — Mussolini's reclaimed Pontine Marshes — 25 years ago on the Anzio Beachhead, and of the enemy hills beyond, laughing at us in the heat. There was a cross-roads between our trenches and the Germans, identified on the map as Femina Morte — the Dead Woman — and all around it that May, for acres, the poppies blossomed, an undulating sea of crimson, fertilized with blood.

It made me think of our fathers, and the poppies that bloomed in another field, in Flanders, only 30 years before, as I directed artillery fire on the sons of their fathers at the cross-roads of Femina Morte.

I feel so sad about the Kopechnes and the Kennedys. Is Camelot a mirage in a field of poppies? Might this superb young senator have rallied the knights against the nuclear dragon and made the difference and halted this march down the road to madness — but for that midsummer road to a night-mare?

Is it possible that the same nation that mustered the sub-lime technology to bounce Apollo off the moon and back can, with one and the same stroke present to mankind such stone-age stupidity?

These are depressing

times, and I for one gain no real satisfaction from rolling in the seductive affluence that is the unhappy lot of us Americans, or burying myself in the cult of escapism, our way of life and our tragedy. All this excess wealth, moldy with too much watering, won't last beyond the winds of autumn, and then it will be winter again. The industrial military-congressional complex will see to that.

Killing after wanton street-killing a rock's heave from the wall-to-wall carpets of the New Boston, murder after wanton murder amidst the defoliated poppies of Vietnam.

And a sweet sleek mackerel, all quivery and shimmery and silvery, pulled from the depths of the Bubbler, the raw vomit retched from the johns of Gloucester into the very heart of Le Beauport, the beautiful harbor.

Pay no attention. Midsummer is the season to get away from it all, to set aside the burdens for awhile, to visit the seashore if you live in the mountains, the mountains if you live by the sea, and to set up your chair on the fire escape if you are lucky enough to have chosen Roxbury, above all other Edens on this earth, for your residence.

The rains and the fogs drench and drip, and springs issue from the stone of Cape Ann, but somehow — why, I cannot explain — our throats are parched.

August 8, 1969

14. Hey, you mollycoddled campus bullyrags!

TRYING TO FIGURE YOU YOUNG radicals, as you call yourselves, it suddenly occurs to me that I used to be one myself. I was a student once, and I dropped out of college, you might say, to embark on the glorious mission of killing Germans. That should qualify me by the violent standards of the now.

It was a great cause, stopping Hitler. As an infantry forward observer, I brought down a rain of bombs, shells and bullets on who knows how many faceless fellow humans, and they returned the compliment. All very high-minded and moral there in the forgotten foxholes of Anzio, where we'd been left to rot by our High Command.

Yes, you mollycoddled campus bullyrags, we gaffers were the radicals of a generation ago, we who fought the Krauts and kamikazes, 16,112,566 of us. And may I add that 291,557 of your fathers and grandfathers and uncles died defending this imperfect American society which you are bent on improving by destroying.

No, you are wrong about me. I detest Agnew's hypocritical bull, and I am not implying that the old sacrifices of my generation excuse our responsibility for the horrible state of affairs today, any more than those of our fathers in the First War excused theirs for the Depression and the rise of the fascist beasts.

I merely observe that before you make history, you must learn it. You're not the first idealists, nor I trust the last, not the first radicals, nor the first to discover that life is loaded with injustice, nor the first to resolve to do something about it.

Rest assured, my hairy co-conspirators for a better world, that the radicals of 25 years hence will probably not burden you, their parents, with the guilt of having sold out the ideals for which your peers expired in the rice paddies of southeast Asia. But they'll find plenty enough else to hang on you, you can count on it.

My second crack at radicalism was 17 years ago as an organizer for the American Newspaper Guild, CIO. I ran a strike in Portland, Maine. We were convinced they meant to bust the union. Our people, 200 of them, walked out when negotiations stalled, but we couldn't shut down the paper.

We tried everything. We even published a competitive daily from scratch. It was war. We put mass picket lines around the plant. They got an injunction, and my lieutenants and I were subpoenaed before the Maine

Supreme Court and charged with "inciting to riot and violence."

One afternoon, I met secretly in a waterfront bar with the agent of a sympathetic and very tough union who offered to raise a goon squad on the wharves to beat up the pressmen who were quite legally crossing our picket lines. I said no thanks, but for a moment, desperate as the situation seemed to us, I was tempted.

After a month on the street, we settled. The union was weakened but not broken. No bombs. No arson. No casualties. The charges of riot and violence were forgotten. Perhaps it didn't prove anything.

Well, I was a young hothead then, and I believed; and this was the movement, the labor movement, and just as honorable as yours. And we were up front in those dark days of Joe McCarthy, though such camp stuff as trying to bend the system without busting it is pretty unexciting now when it is so much simpler to get high and burn a building, drown out the guy at the mike or bomb a police station.

The funny thing is that I'm as "radical" today (which would have been "liberal" 20 years ago) as most of the SDS, because I believe in immediate and total withdrawal from Vietnam and amnesty for the evaders of an illegal war draft, an absolute halt to ABM and SST, drastic cuts in defense spending, admission of China to the UN, electoral reform, equal rights for blacks, women, fishermen and all other oppressed groups, free speech, prosecution of all polluters except myself, national health insurance, and nationalization of the rails, public utilities and the oil industry. I also happen to believe in life imprisonment for the unreconstructible enemies of society.

You half-baked, self-styled, self-righteous, free-living, free-loving, freeloading "radicals" haven't even started to earn the title by my standards. You're not radicals. You're juvenile delinquents, and so you deserve to be treated until you shape up and recognize that slow and frustrating as it is, it's the only system, the only social order we have, and for lack of better, the best the world has ever seen.

This old land of the free is having trouble enough with the Nixons and Agnews and Mitchells, the war, the gun lobby, the oil lobby, the racists, profiteers, panthers, poverty, polluters, the Middle East, Russia, China, the pushers, the Mafia, the hard hats and the know-nothings and the do-nothings without the rear-guard harassments of a guerrilla gang of spoiled kiddoes who think the world is their rumpus room.

I know you're not listening, but how about it, boys and girls — won't you get with it and join the human race while you're still eligible?

October 2, 1970

The Long Haul

Jack McKay was typical of the old-time Bluenose fishermen who for generations moved to Gloucester from Nova Scotia for new opportunities and a new life, giving far more than they got in the bargain. His warmhearted wife Josephine (Josie), a Prince Edward Islander, was our housekeeper for a while.

15. WHEN FISH WERE FISH AND MEN WERE MEN

TWAS FOUR DAYS BEFORE CHRIST-mas of 1916 that Jack McKay sailed for Newfoundland after a load of frozen herring for bait. His Pa was skipper. He minds it well.

Jack's mother died when he was three and Auntie brought him up. Then he quit Glouces-ter High School and went down to Bucksport, Maine, to go on the schooner *Elizabeth N.* with his father at 30 bucks a month, half the crew's wage. He was 15.

Last year Jack retired as as-sistant engineer on the US fish-ery research vessel *Delaware*. So now this gentle bulldog fisher-man of the old school has time enough to stroll down from his snug house at 74 Eastern Av-enue for his daily visit with the cronies at the Elks and along the waterfront, what's left of it. And to recollect the way it was.

Every Christmastime re-

Jack and Josie McKay

minds him of that trip with his father, Captain Jack McKay, the first bulldog, bushy-browed, who came up from Guysboro, Nova Scotia, in 1883 to become one of the famous old Glouces-ter skippers, all now gone.

And since this is the sea-son of miracles, what could be more to the point than to pause in our story to tell of the mira-cle of Captain Jack, senior, and his brother, known far and wide as Little Bill?

Young Jack had already gone with his Pa halibuting on the Grand Bank a couple of summers in the schooner *Monitor* as "catchy," meaning he was just along to learn, assigned to catch the painters, the bow lines, of the dories as they came alongside after setting their trawls.

It was this same *Monitor* that Captain McKay took past Eastern Point on March 4, 1908, bound for the Grand Bank. With him were two brothers, Fred and Charlie, and son Willie. Jack was in school then.

Captain McKay's third brother, Little Bill, was on the Bank already with Captain Bob Porper in the *Cavalier.*

In spite of dirty weather, Captain Jack kept a press of canvas and the *Monitor* made the run of 800 miles in jig time. When they reached the edge of the grounds it was blowing hard norwest. Then out of nowhere the schooner came on the first of a line of dories, having a bad time of it hauling trawl in the sharp seas.

"That's Porper's gang!" somebody yelled, recognizing the *Cavalier's* gear.

"Well whaddya know, I guess we'll run down the line and speak to Little Bill," the skipper observed coolly.

They jogged along without sighting another, when the lookout called: "Hey Skipper, there's a dory ahead, bottom up with a couple o' men hanging on!"

Captain McKay ordered a dory swung in the slings, and while it dropped over the side and the men pulled away, he reached for his glasses. As they bent to their oars, he cried: "Drive her boys, for God's sake! That's Little Bill on the stern there, and he's near all in!"

The weather was that bad it was two days before the rescued dorymates could be put back aboard the *Cavalier*, and there was talk enough for a long while after about whatever it was that had told Captain Jack to drive her so hard, just in time after 800 miles to pluck Little Bill from the deep.

So this was the man the boy Jack put to sea under, four days before Christmas of 1916.

The *Elizabeth N.* pushed along to the eastward, and a bitterly Christmas it was on board, and then across Cabot Strait and

into the Bay of Islands on the wintry northwest coast of Newfoundland. Two other schooners had preceded them, and they commenced taking aboard the frozen herring, bought from the natives.

"Well," says Jack, "we got her loaded all right and started to get under way fast as we could, but the ice beat us to it, all three vessels. We stayed on board for a week while it froze solid, and that's where I spent my 16th birthday.

"Then the whole gang of us walked across the ice up the Bay and 10 or 15 miles up the Humber River, froze too — hard country, I'll tell you — to a place called Curling. Hung around there four days in a savage storm waiting for the narrow gauge to plow in.

"Took the train along the coast to Port-aux-Basques. Hung around for the icebreaker *Kyle* and went on board of her and bucked across to North Sydney. She'd back off, give it a crack, then back off again — what a jolt! Then we took the train back to Bucksport."

Once more in Gloucester, young Jack went catchy with Captain Porper in the *Cavalier*, and while they were on the Grand Bank, America entered the war. Nineteen days later, on April 25, a German U-boat put Captain McKay's old *Monitor*, since sold, on the bottom of the Mediterranean, on her way back from taking fish to Italy.

In a few weeks the *Cavalier* sailed into the Bay of Islands, and young Jack saw the *Elizabeth N.* and the others just thawing out.

In due course the Old Man went down with his crew and sailed her home, rounding out his broken trip with a load of frozen herring.

II

SHE'S GONE AND LONG FORGOTTEN now, but in the first flush of her youth *Hesper* was the queen of the pilot schooners, the fastest in America. Jack sailed on her last trip.

What a sweet one she was! Dennison Lawlor, the great designer, built her at East Boston in 1884, long and fine and radically deep, and from the day she was launched for the Boston pilots they knew they had something extra in this plumb stem beauty.

Nobody could touch her. All had a go at it, every spanking new fisherman and yacht and she showed 'em all her wake. The best match though, and among the worst lickings *Hesper* ever gave, was the very first of the fishermen's races, the one no one seems to know about today — first because it was sailed fully six years before Gloucester's famous "Race that Blew" in 1892, won by the *Harry L. Belden.*

Some fish dealers and yachtsmen put up a cup and a $400 purse for a Boston fishermen's race to be sailed on May 1, 1886, outside the Harbor. These were the days when designers like Lawlor and McManus and Burgess and Crowninshield were beginning to mold their genius into the fast lines of the fishing schooners, because the fastest and first to market got the big prices.

Now the Boston fishing fleet wanted no part of *Hesper,* Pilot Boat No 5. Too yachtlike, they claimed. But a compromise was finally reached, allowing her to qualify for the cup only. And to their later sorrow, they let her carry a jib topsail over the canvas permitted the rest of the starting fleet of eleven schooners.

It was a 33-mile triangular course as far out as Halfway Rock. The air was light — too light, the fishermen complained afterwards. *Hesper* slipped across the finish for the cup, over four miles ahead of her nearest rival, the *John H. McManus,* which took the purse.

No, they never could touch her in her heyday and *Hesper* influenced the design of the fleet and the pilot boats and yachts for years to come.

The *Roseway* is about the last of the old style pilots now, and she's a sight to see coming down from Boston to Gloucester a couple of times a year for overhaul, though no longer under sail.* Too bad *Hesper's* influence hasn't stretched to the current model being used by the Gloucester and Salem pilots, which resembles a half-sunk tugboat going backwards.

But to return to *Hesper* and

---

* *Roseway* was put up for sale by the Boston Pilots in 1975, bought by partners Jim Sharp and Orvil Young, and converted back to a handsome sailing schooner, windjamming out of Camden, Maine, with their great Gloucester fishing schooner *Adventure,* which Captain Sharp gave to the people of Gloucester in 1988. *Roseway* continues in the passenger cruise trade under another owner in 1994.

The Boston pilot schooner
Hesper, *Gloucester Harbor*

Jack McKay, who when last heard from was wryly observing his 16th birthday frozen in the Newfoundland ice with his Pa aboard the schooner *Elizabeth N.*

After learning the ropes with Captain Bob Porper on the *Cavalier,* the kid, all of 18, signed on the old *Hesper,* now a fisherman out of Bucksport, Maine, stripped of her outside ballast keel for the price of the lead, bound south from Gloucester with the mackerel seining fleet. Captain George Hodsdon was skipper and Uncle Bill McKay was mate, the same lucky Little Bill.

During the night of May 4 they were running into Delaware Bay to get the mackerel news at Lewes when it breezed up from the southeast.

"'We were trying to get in around Delaware Breakwater," Jack recalls, "but we couldn't keep her away, and off Cape Henlopen we run her ashore on a sand bar. Torched off a flare, and in a while the lifesavers pushed out in their boat after us.

"By then we could feel old *Hesper* starting to break up right under us, so we took to the seine boat — saved the seine too — and rowed up the Delaware all 16 of us, like General Washington, up to the lifesaving station at Lewes."

Some of the bunch stayed there, but most were taken in at the telegraph office, where the operator let them sleep on the floor after closing time.

He was a good fellow, that operator, because none of them had the price of a train ticket, and he loaned it on their say-so. Jack remembers it yet — $16.60. Home in Gloucester he borrowed from his sister and paid the man back, as did all but one of the rest.

Around five years ago the Gloucester research vessel

Delaware chanced to put into Lewes, for equipment. Assistant Engineer Jack McKay, strolling around town, was recognized and hailed by none other than the man who saw their flare and called the lifesavers.

So all was not forgotten after all, and now the world can know that *Hesper* died proper and was buried fittin' — as a good queen should.

III

PUSHING HIS 21ST BIRTHDAY IN 1922, Jack was fresh-halibuting with Captain Peter Dunsky in the Gloucester schooner *Republic* down off the coast of Newfoundland.

Joe Johnson was his dorymate. They were hauling trawl, a mile of it. The weather wasn't bad but bitter, and the work was a backbreaker. The schooner lay a ways off. The other dories were strung out across the water, hauling too.

"By Jeez!" grunted Johnson, batting a big halibut on the nose, "d'ye know the course into St. Pierre? To hell with this — let's put up the sail and get outa here."

They were on what's called Hawkins Spot, St. Pierre Bank, and Joe must have been

right fed up to propose sailing an 18-foot open banks dory the 80 or 90 miles into the French island.

Jack ground away at the hurdy-gurdy clamped athwartships to the gunwales, winching in the heavy trawl. He didn't look up. "Are you nuts, Joe? Forget it! C'mon, let's finish up and get aboard for mug-up." Which they did, rowing back to the *Republic*, Joe Johnson muttering all the while.

That evening it breezed up, and the schooner was blown clear down to Burgeo. No dory would have stood a chance.

Hard times and hard men. Take this Dunsky, a native Russian, and a bear. One day in the spring of '18 *Republic's* main boom knocked him clean overboard in the height of a storm. His men launched a dory in its teeth, pulled him out by the scruff of his neck, got him back aboard, squeezed a gallon of ocean from him and in a few hours he was up on deck.

What was the worst of it, Jack, in the days when men were men?

McKay lights a cigarette, scrunches up that bulldog face: "Dory trawling. The fear of get-

ting separated from the vessel, going adrift. All the skipper had for instruments was lead, log and barometer and your life hung on what the glass said, whether to put the dories over or not.

"But the thing we were most scared of was the ice in the winter. That spray would strike and freeze, and the snow and sleet, clear up to the mastheads, all caked on spars, sails, rigging. Why you'd be so topheavy there'd be times she'd roll when you'd think she wasn't going to stand up again. Ice took plenty to the bottom.

"On the other side of it, when you come to riding out a gale of wind there was nothing to beat a schooner. She'd just jog along right nice and easy under jumbo and reefed foresail, when your beam trawler was rolling rail under."

The crowning moment under sail for Jack McKay, like all the rest, came during the Fishermen's Races.

This was the end of August 1923, a special race for the 50th anniversary of the incorporation of the City of Gloucester. The prize was a cup from Sir Thomas Lipton and Colonel

John Prentiss and a purse of $2,400. The Tea King, who tried so many times so valiantly with his series of *Shamrocks* for the America's Cup, was there, and so was Mayor John F. (Honey Fitz) Fitzgerald of Boston, President Kennedy's grandfather.

Three schooners were entered: *Shamrock,* in honor of Sir Thomas, Captain Marty Welch, just launched; Captain Ben Pine's snowwhite *Elizabeth Howard* and Captain Clayt Morrissey's *Henry Ford,* only a year old.

Mainmastheadman on the *Ford* was none other than Jack McKay, standing away up there on the crosstrees, 65 feet above the deck, clinging to shroud or halyard, a loftier twin to the foremastheadman, looking from afar like insects in the twigs.

The job of the mastheadman was to handle the high end of the setting or the taking in of the great topsails and the fisherman's staysail, and a ticklish proposition it was to inch through the rigging monkey fashion, one hand for the vessel and one for yourself, the wind screeching, your perch whipping like a fishpole.

But Jack was the man for it, a fisherman-sailor with the daredevil of youth.

The first match was called on account of light air. But the next day it blew, and Clayt sailed the able *Henry Ford,* with McKay at his mainmasthead, to snatch the cup and the cash from Ben Pine and the *Howard,* Marty Welch's *Shamrock* a poor third, perhaps not yet in trim.

Jack was in the freighters, then learned machinist ashore in Gloucester, went engineer with Captain Frank Favalora on the *Grace F,* got his chief's papers, shipped on the Boston beam trawlers, landing with Captain Iver Carlson on the *Wave.*

When the Navy made the *Wave* a Q Boat in World War II, Jack rose to lieutenant. After the war, back to the Boston and Gloucester draggers, winding up with nine years as assistant engineer in the US Fisheries Research Vessel *Delaware* until retirement in '66.

He'd do it all over again, he says, the better part of 50 years at sea . . . "must be the salt in the blood, or the air, or something."

He loves Gloucester. He is Gloucester. Jack McKay's the

kind of man, thousands of them, who made her great.

December 22 & 27, 1967;
January 5, 1968

16. FORMER WHARF RAT REVEALS HIDDEN HOARD OF MEMORIES ～w～

THERE'S A YARN JIM CONNOLLY cranked out right after the turn of the century, "From Reykjavik to Gloucester", about a cocksure English yachtsman who challenged a Gloucester fisherman to an ocean race.

The story is told from the "Crow's Nest" which was a familiar lookout tower atop one of the fish companies, with a fine illustration of the men sitting about, keeping an eye on the schooners sailing in around Eastern Point.

Charlie McPhee is one of the elder statesmen of the waterfront now, and having quit the sea, bunks up in back of the Diner off Chestnut Street where he has his own good view of his old harbor and can spin off a yarn of yore when so moved. He remembers those crow's nests well.

"Up in Harbor Cove," says he, "most all of the fish compa-

nies, I'd say, had these glassed-in rooms on their roofs, like widow's walks, and each of 'em had the best doryman they could get for the job.

"He'd climb up every now and then and keep watch for the schooners coming in round the Breakwater. Course they were so familiar, you know, that a good man could recognize 'em all just by their mastheads, from that far.

"So the first glimpse of the first of the fleet coming round, down the stairs they run and jump into the dories and race out into the harbor to be the first to buy a trip of fish. Best price to the lead vessel, of course."

There were all sorts of specialists on the water in those times. Charlie recollects the streamers, the dorymen who made their living rowing around to each vessel where she lay in

Charlie McPhee

The Crow's Nest

the stream, just in, and they'd buy up the cook's grease, old spent rope and such odds and ends from the living at sea, and the wear and tear of it.

Paddy Carr was a familiar figure for decades, oaring from vessel to vessel to collect the fish livers for rendering into vitamins, and woe to him who tried to pass off one from a mackerel shark.

Then there were maybe a half a dozen men, recalls Charlie, the gaffers.

"Nobody ever horned in on those boys, I'll tell you. They had it all to themselves by a kind of an unspoken understanding along the waterfront.

"They had long gaffs, that's where the name come from, and they'd hang around in their dories while the vessels were unloading. They'd gaff all the fish that chanced to fall overboard and before you'd know it a man would have a doryload. Nope, nothin' much went to waste in them days."

Charlie was born in '97 in the block his family owned next east on Main Street to the North Shore Automotive. His pa was Captain Sylvanus McPhee.

His grandma, Mrs. Joanna Prior, did so well running a boardinghouse for fishermen that she got to own shares in some of the vessels, and she helped raise money for Howard Blackburn after he came back to Gloucester from Newfoundland, lacking his frozen fingers, in 1883.

A regular wharf rat was Charlie. When he was nothing but a sprite his first chore first thing in the morning was to take the dory and scrounge up firewood for his uncle, a Civil War veteran whose place still stands down there back of the North Shore Theater, and then he'd help the old man mend nets.

"Wish I'd stayed in school," muses Charlie. "But I hated book learning, and quit in 1913. Howard Blackburn had his bar just a couple of doors down the street, and I used to run errands for him, so he signed my papers to get into the Mass Maritime Academy, on the training ship.

"He was some man, Captain Blackburn. Weekends sometimes in the summer I'd crew for him, and we'd sail his little sloop down to Boston or P-town or up to the Shoals. He said he always felt better when he was out on the water. Seemed to make his poor maimed hands and feet easier.

"Anyways, old Granny Lane was my teacher at the Sawyer School. Gawd, she was so feeble they had to bring her back and forth in a carriage.

"But every summer vacation, I don't know how she did it, she'd take a trip to some different part of the world, and when she got back and school opened don't you think us kids had a ball for a while because Granny'd forget the books and spend the whole class telling us about the places she'd been.

"The year after I quit Sawyer, that would be in '14, the training ship put into Naples, and I went down and saw the ruins of Pompeii, and something moved me to send Granny a picture postcard.

"Well, I heard later that she was some proud. She read that card to the class, and then she waggled her finger at 'em the

way she always did and said: 'Charlie's a hellion, but he'll make a man of himself yet.' "

Hellion? He raised some hell during Prohibition as a rum-runner, I know that, because he told me some stories that would raise the hair right off the back of your head. But he wouldn't let me write them — afraid they'd spoil his image with his grandchildren.

Prohibition was repealed with the coming of the New Deal in 1933. There were fifteen million unemployed in America. Still, Charlie and his old buddy Anthony (Monk) Sears were able to eke out a living jigging and netting in Charlie's Jonesport 40-footer *Canopus,* which he named after his father's fishing vessel.

But they were growing weary of the unending hard work, and these were restless times. Looking at a map one August day, it occurred to them that the whole of the US east of the Mississippi is one big island. Why not shake the salt of Gloucester off their tails, run a ring around it in *Canopus,* and see for themselves how half the country was doing?

II

IT HAPPENED THAT 1933 WAS THE year of the World's Fair at Chicago, and Captain Ben Pine was fitting out the schooner *Gertrude L. Thebaud* to take her up there as the Massachusetts exhibit, going by way of the St. Lawrence River.

Did Piney spose there might be something in the way of work helping out if they were to meet him in Chicago on their own hook? Sure, he laughed, thinking they'd play out before they ever got there in a little 40-footer.

So Charlie and Monk put grub aboard, pocketed what small cash they had and set out. They ran down to New York and then chugged up through the Hudson River, real pretty countryside along there, but when they struck the Erie Canal in upstate New York the man told them at Lock Number 1 that he couldn't be bothered to let 'em through unless they passed in company with a larger vessel.

"We waited around and waited around," Charlie run his fingers through that white thatch of hair, "and time dragged, I'll say. It was mighty slow going,

cause there were 33 locks in all.

"So after we'd gone through six or eight of 'em along with a bigger boat, we got to Oswego and got ahold of a chart, and sure enough, by taking the piddling little Oswego Canal, just a runoff, we could get out to Lake Ontario and sneak around all the rest of the canal. Which we did."

A man had to work any angle he could in those days of the Great Depression, and when they got to the Welland Canal on the Canadian side of Niagara, the keeper said it would cost 15 bucks to go through to Lake Erie, but if they could get a tow he wouldn't charge a nickel.

"We weren't what you'd call overburdened with money, and we argued, but 'twas no good. We tied up there, and the steamers and towboats and everything else went right by and wouldn't give us the time of day, so we had to pay up after all.

"Come out at Port Colborne, steamed through the Erie and up by Detroit into Lake Huron, and when we put into Alpena, Michigan, what do you spose we tied up alongside of but an old iron gillnetter that had gone out from Michigan to

Gloucester when that bunch of bears went salt water fishing and settled, you know, and then this one had gone back for some reason.

"We had towed a dory all this way and got so sick of the damn thing that after we'd come down Lake Michigan and made Benton Harbor right above Chicago and a kid come along and fell in love with it and just had to have it, well, he had a couple of bucks, and we were pretty desperate for money, so we let him take it off our hands."

What a sight for Gloucester eyes at Chicago! There on the lake shore, the towering topmasts of the *Thebaud*, tied up already at the vast Navy Pier, and the Fair crowds streaming aboard her.

Captain Pine and crew were taken aback to see *Canopus* drift up alongside, never expected they'd make it, but pleased too, and work of a sort for the pair was found.

Fifteen miles down the lake at the Fair Grounds was the Lunenburg schooner *Bluenose*, *Thebaud's* somewhat rancorous Nova Scotian racing rival, and when she left, the Gloucesterman took her berth.

Guglielmo Marconi arrived one day with a fanfare, and a grand gala was worked up, the feature of which was to be a lake excursion in some tycoon's steam yacht, with a fancy luncheon and testimonials to the great Italian inventor of radio.

"Course we're there in *Canopus*, taking all this in," Charlie recalls, "and the last speech is made, and a roar goes up from the crowd, and they jangle the engine room, and there's a blast on the whistle.

"The engineer gives her some steam, and the screw starts to turn, and with the first revolution one of the blades drops off. Boy!

"Now Monk was a great swimmer, you know. He stripped down, dove in with a line, and he found that blade on the bottom, tied his rope on and surfaced.

"They hauled the blade up, and some divers got it back on the propeller in hardly any time at all.

"Well, old Marconi was watching all the while, and he was so tickled with Monk's performance that he gave him a slap on the back and fifteen bucks."

III

"ONE FINE DAY," RECOLLECTS Charlie, "they were having these long distance swimming races over the 15 miles from the Navy Pier to the World's Fair Pier, sponsored by William Randolph Hearst.

"What a time! They came from all over the world to enter. And big crowds. So we thought we'd follow along in *Canopus*. They fired off the gun and there was a helluva splash when the contestants dove in off the pier — a right queer-looking bunch — and began thrashing out into the lake.

"After a bit we got tired of it, and just as we were turning back Monk spotted something away offshore. We steamed out, quite some distance, and what d'you spose?

"It was a lady swimmer name of Carmichael who held the American women's endurance record, I believe. My God, she must have weighed 300 pounds, and covered with grease from head to toe, to keep warm you know.

"She was right cheerful and told us she'd been hurt at the start when some Russian or somebody jumped in and landed on her stomach. Too hurt to swim, but she couldn't sink either and was blown out by the offshore breeze.

"We tried to get her aboard, but cripes she was so heavy, and slippery as a hippo in a mudhole, that neither she nor us could make any headway."

Charlie had to chuckle.

"So what do you think we did? We tied a line around, under her arms, and we towed her all the way back to the pier — a couple of miles it must have been anyway — keeping her close by our quarter so she'd stay clear of the propellor.

"Of course the word had spread, and when we got there the Coast Guard was waiting, and they had a crane down on the pier. After we docked they just put a strap around our lady, real easy like, and hoisted her out of Lake Michigan and took her to the hospital."

Charlie, you're putting me on.

"Nossir I ain't. It's the truth and nothing but. The whole story is just the way it happened!"

By October the Fair was winding up, time to move on.

Charlie McPhee aboard Canopus

Louis where the worst was, there were thousands and thousands of folks who'd been put off the land and out of their homes.

"A lot of them were living on these broken-down house-boats, if they were lucky. Why, the banks of the river for hundreds of miles were crawling with shantytowns, people living in packing boxes and culverts and under bridges and in cardboard shacks.

"It was the most awful thing I ever saw, right here in the United States, terrible. It's a nightmare to me yet, after all these years.

"Shucks, when we left Chicago we were almost sunk with the food Piney give us, and we passed that stuff out to folks all along that river trip, good people, you know, good citizens, working people flat broke and starving.

"Being able to do that, just being able to do some little thing for a few of them — that was the best part of the whole damn trip, and when we reached New Orleans we'd put one helluva dent in that grub."

To bypass the long run down the Delta, *Canopus* slipped through the small-craft canal at

The *Thebaud*, too, was fixing to leave, and she was so well stocked with food, especially canned goods which various companies had given her owners as a promotion, that Captain Pine told Charlie and Monk to take all they could carry aboard *Canopus*.

They left Chicago following the same route Howard Blackburn had taken from Gloucester 30 years earlier in his sloop *Great Republic* through the canal system linking Lake Michigan to the Illinois River and then down to join the great Mississippi above St. Louis.

"You know, we thought we'd seen hard times, but it was nothing to what we saw down on that river," muses Charlie. "The whole way down the Mississippi, but especially below St.

Violet, Louisiana, into Lake Borgne and out to the Gulf of Mexico.

Along the Gulf coast they steamed staying pretty close inshore as they had nothing but the crudest kind of a chart aboard.

They were poking along off Pensacola, Florida, one afternoon, taking in the scenery of the semitropics, when Monk let out a shout:

"What the heck's that, over the palm trees there — don't tell me them's mastheads!"

Charlie craned his neck and gave a squint and cut the engine and whooped: "You ain't kiddin' them are mastheads — and Gloucester vessels, I'd know 'em anywhere! C'mon Monk, let's go see!"

IV

HE PUT THE WHEEL HARD OVER, and they nosed about until they found a passage around what turned out to be a palmstudded key.

Behind it, in the lee of the lagoon, lay a fleet of maybe 40 Gloucester schooners, anchored in rafts of two or three abreast, and not a sign of life about any of them, nor a sound to be heard but the sighing of the breeze through the rigging, the creaking of the tackle and the gentle lapping of wavelets against the dark topsides of the handsome vessels.

But hark! Away down at the end of the lagoon, on board of the farthermost vessel, they catch the tiny figure of a man waving. On deck with him is a dog.

Canopus chugs down through the silent fleet.

Who should it turn out to be but an old friend from back home, Frank Cooney, left there as watchman while the rest of the crews are ashore, and was he glad to see them!

Sure enough, they were all from Gloucester, holed in there, waiting out the hurricane season to go snapper fishing.

Charlie was hard up for a chart of the Florida waters, so Frank obligingly dug around and produced a spare — a real antique in fact, published in 1885 and so out of date that Miami was identified merely as Cape Florida.

But that didn't matter. They said goodbye and we'll see you and steamed into Pensacola where they found a berth. Plenty of that grub from the *Thebaud*

left, but not much money.

"Next morning," Charlie minds it well, "Monk and me were up forward in the cuddy, watching the coffee water come to a boil — I've always been a great coffee hound — and somebody gives us a holler.

"We stick our snouts out the companionway and who the heck d'you think it is up there peering down at us but old Skatey Doran?

"Cripes, I knew him right off. He'd come down here to the beaches and got sand in his boots, as they say, and he saw the name and the hail on our stern as he was passing: *CANO-PUS* Gloucester.

"Oh, he was a gruff old bird, you know, and he growls at us: 'Gloucester, Mass.?' And we said yup.

"*Canopus*, huh?

'Yup.

"'*Canopus* from Gloucester. Wal, she sure shrunk a lot.'

"That was all. Old Skatey, the last *Canopus* he ever laid eyes on was my pa's *Canopus* that he'd sailed in, the big boat I'd named my little one after."

Coasting down to St. Petersburg, they put in there, and like everywhere else they had made port on their long and mostly inland passage from Cape Ann, they had to tell the whole story of it all over again to the curious — and in these bitterly hard times there was a surplus of folks with nothing else to do but pass the time of day.

Anyway, at St. Pete's the Coast Guard officer boarded them, and when he spotted the old chart from Frank Cooney his eyes popped. He just had to have it and offered them a brand new series for the entire Gulf and Atlantic coasts if they'd swap.

This ploy put Charlie wise, and he figured his dog-eared source of misinformation must be worth something at that, so he wouldn't give it up, nossir.

For a time they fished for snappers, and then they steamed on to Miami and spent the rest of the winter taking parties sportfishing.

By springtime the homing urge grew strong, and Charlie and Monk shook the sands of Miami out of their boots and worked their way up along the east coast.

In June of 1934 *Canopus* rounded the Breakwater and slipped home. Ten months and 6,000 miles to show what a cinch it was for two Gloucester fishermen to circumnavigate the eastern half of the United States in a 40-foot Jonesport fishing boat — in the middle of the Great Depression with nothing much but their wits to live on.

A year or so later, time and tide being what they are, Charlie McPhee sold *Canopus* to parties now unremembered.

The worst of it was, he clean forgot that his priceless old chart was still aboard — until she was long gone.

July 1, 3, 5 and 22, 1968

17. God rest ye, merry fishermen! ⟋⟍

MERRY CHRISTMAS, YE MERRY fishermen of Gloucester. Greetings, and may providence repent, and reprieve you to hang on 'til yet another birthday of the Fisher of Men comes round.

Do ye remember your First Christmas here? I do. It was 345 of them ago, and I am looking out the warm room through the double glass window and across the wind-skittered, blue-cold stretch of harbor to Stage Head where you celebrated it.

Celebrated, did I say? You miserable lot, the fourteen of you planted there to catch fish for the rich men who staked you, left to live off the land the rest of the year, you scrimy, dirty, lice-crawling, ragged, scurvied, half-starved, three-quarters frozen collection of damn fools from the English coast.

What a jolly Christmas that was, eh? Bunched in your lean-to there between the wilderness and the wicked sea, the Arctic wind blasting through every chink, huddled around the fire, stamping your frostbit feet, gagging on the smoke and swigging the rotgut the rest had left you when they hied back to Blighty for more supplies, cursing the Dorchester merchants who sent you here (so plump and comfy with their wives and little ones, toasting their backsides at the hearthsides, with their Madeira and their fat geese and their blood puddings), and trying not to curse your God, too, for leaving you to such a fate on this Christmas of 1623, all forsaken in the land of savages on a God-forsaken rock called Cape Ann.

Like fools, you hung on, but after two more such Merry Christmases your ill-planned, ill-commanded, ill-equipped, ill-manned, ill-starred expedition collapsed in bankruptcy. The wise ones sailed home, leaving a few bullheads to straggle farther along with Roger Conant to what somebody said were the greener fields of Naumkeag.

Old John White, the man of God who set you in motion and kept you alive without ever leaving England, watched from 3,000 miles away and reflected: "First, no sure fishing place in the land is fit for planting, nor any good place for planting found fit for fishing, at least, near the shore; and, secondly, rarely any fisherman will work at land; neither are husbandmen fit for fishermen, but with long use and experience."

Oh I remember you, you first fishermen — and it was the first and only time that you and the rest that came after you ever

---

49

gave up on this place. And you, do you know that it was you created the Bay Colony of Massachusetts, and Massachusetts the Revolution, and the Revolution America? And fed it and fattened it on salt fish?

In 1879, for an example, 429 schooners brought in 40,133,000 pounds of cod, 13,212,000 pounds of halibut, 48,643 barrels of mackerel and 20,000 of herring. The price: 29 schooners, 249 lives, 57 widows and 140 fatherless children.

On it went, from father to son: fish, rum, slaves, sugar, molasses, lumber, cotton, dollars, vessels for trading, vessels for fishing, fish for salt, salt for fish, fish for duck, fish for hemp, fish for hooks, fish for bait, fish for Gloucester, for roads, for houses, for stores, for derby hats, for taxes, for whisky, for City Halls, for wharves, for schools, for summer people, for drugstores, for tourists, for cars, fish for lives, fish for more fishermen.

Merry Christmas, fishermen. Everything Gloucester is, barely proud yet, the once biggest fishing port in the world, you made her. Everything.

Fishermen, you are Gloucester, you antiheroes, you fished-out species. Why do you hang on to embarrass a hostile world, glaring at your extinction like fish hawks?

They've all had a crack at you. First the French, then the English, and the Canadians (the old rivalry for the grounds and the markets, your brothers, who can blame them?) . . . and your own fish-built country (your last Federal friend John Adams, 1783), the short buyers and the long sellers, the Russians, the Japs, Greenland, Iceland, Scandinavia . . . and the old enemy, riding higher than ever, strutting the deck of your new, antiquated factory ship, telling you dummkopfen how dey do idt in Germany (using your old Marshall Plan taxes that came out of the hold and the dollars they draw off mid dere zo efficient liddle reefers bringing fish slabs into Gloucester.)

And always the sea . . . waiting.

Merry Christmas, you less-than-merry fishermen of Gloucester every one, and all your families.

And hang on, for Gloucester's sake, hang on.

December 20, 1968

Three columns between mid-1969 and mid-1971 reflect the accelerating decline of the fisheries and the morale of the fishermen pushed, if not brought on, by the all-out assault of foreign factory fleets on "distant waters", most notably Georges Bank. The Gloucester guys were not above reproach; but they vied for their share, as one of them told me as if in a daze, against "an armada of foreigners from horizon to horizon, like a World War Two convoy." At that, no one dared dream that as soon as 1994 the Northwest Atlantic fishery would verge on extinction.

18. STAND TOGETHER, MEN, OR FALL APART ⎯⎯

A HUNDRED AND THIRTY YEARS AGO Amos Story and Jeff Rowe of East Gloucester would row out, and in a few hours catch a doryload, mind you, of fat haddock between Niles Beach and Ten Pound Island.

Some comedown. Today Gloucester's main course is all but wiped out by greed and recklessness, and the government is trying to figure what to do about it.

Once again, the same old story. Either no supply, or no market. Halibut schooled so thick on Georges in the 1830's that men merely leaned over the side and gaffed them aboard. Now, for practical purposes, exterminated.

And mackerel, an immense catch here once. But no one eats salt mackerel any more, and no one's bothered to find a better way to preserve them.

Hence, though they're on a cyclical upswing, the market's so thin that for every one of this fragile delicacy that winds up on a dinner plate, a thousand are mashed into fertilizer or dumped.

Whiting . . . crazy prices. Codfish . . . steadier, but when the salting ceased, it lost its salty savor.

Swordfish, once a moneymaker here, and tuna . . . they inhabit the world of sports now. Redfish . . . boom — and bust. Good old greysole's good when you find him. Lobster . . . overfished. Clams . . . polluted and overdug. As for dogfish . . . the minute a use for the ugly buggers is discovered, they'll disappear, you can count on that.

Now the Bureau of Commercial Fisheries* wants to promote the pollock fishery, and we'll see how long that one lasts

before we zap it.

Against our history of depletion, neglect, political weakness and the effects of ruinous foreign competition, doesn't the future of what's left of the Gloucester fisheries (if they have one) lie in opening up a national market for that most subtle of culinary delights and healthful of proteins, the fresh-caught denizen of the North Atlantic?

Everyone pays lip service to the idea that our remaining species must be protected and developed in a planned manner.

And yet, how will we go after the pollock? In the old way, every boat for itself, racing to the kill, leaving prices to the dealers, with regard to neither market security nor conservation until one more species has been fished out?

Or will our fishermen at

* Now the National Marine Fisheries Service

last wise up, and wake up to the bad dream that after 350 years they are finally staring extinction in the face unless they put aside their small differences and some of their vaunted supposed independence and organize a co-operative? Many of the points for a producers' co-op are plain enough, and their economies — joint purchasing of fuel, food, ice, twine, gear and so forth, jointly-owned take-out, storage and trucking facilities, and more face-to-face confrontation with the retail market.

The Terrasini clan behind the Gloucester Marine Railways, with their attorney, City Councilor Miles Schlichte, have been working in this direction for some time, with the idea that their repair yards and family-connected fleet are in the strongest position in the city to form a co-op. Good luck to them.

There are other points. One was tossed at me a while back by Al Bezanson before he left the BCF. Al saw the stock boat as the answer to creeping rot and the sea cock, carelessly left open. He dreamed of a fleet of smallish (maybe 55 feet), fast, efficiently fished market vessels, leanly crewed and built at con-siderable savings by production methods like ferro-cement.

Identical hulls, power plants, fishing gear, electronic stuff . . . bulk bought, interchangeable parts, real efficient service. Impossible? Not if the men will get together.

The strongest not-so-visible argument for a fishermen's cooperative is by far the most significant. That's market development. Nobody is lifting a finger to promote a national demand for fresh fish. I mean fresh. Bezanson, again, showed with his plastic and foam container that fish can be flown around the world and remain as fresh as when caught.

The BCF has come up with the know-how to put sea-fresh fish on millions of American tables. It remains for private enterprise to get them there by opening the eyes of the American housewife to the scrumptious delights of man's finest, all-round nutritional food.

Our leading processors seem disinclined to travel this road. So private enterprise, here at home, means a fishermen's co-op with the pooled capital to hire food specialists, market analysts and a smart ad agency to create the bright package and the irresistible image that will sell fish to America, fresh off the boats to the cry of the gull and the groan of the Whistler and so on. A good place to start would be the regional supermarket chain.

If the Madison Avenue boys can kill underarm odor, glue down dentures and stop stomach rumble, they ought to have a field day with the most exciting food discovery to dazzle the nation since Clarence Birdseye put us back on the map.

Fresh cusk and white shrimp in Cheyenne . . . mackerel, pollock and yellowtail in KC . . . ocean catfish, sole and cod in Albuquerque.

But no boat can do it alone.

June 27, 1969

19. THE DEVIL'S MARK IS ON THE HADDOCK ~~~

OVER THE PAST FOURTEEN GENER-ations or so fishing has reaped an abundance of anguish for Gloucester, along with some small good for all I know, and it seems destined to continue so, since those who live by the sea live by the whim of it.

We are losers and always have been. Losers, long-shot gamblers playing ridiculous odds against the sea, the all-powerful, the ever-resourceful sea, for the penny ante of her fish against the penny ante of our lives. But such good losers. The world loves us.

And now a New Year creeps out of the crib of the horizon, already whiskered with cynicism. And once more the odds have shifted. The new stake in the old game is no longer the fish but the players — the sea and the race of man.

There is a melancholy about the fishing here, a fore-boding, symbolic and mysterious as the prey is. Gloucester has been too much striving, for too little, at too much cost. The devil's mark, so says the legend, is on the haddock. Fishermen are poets without tongue, artists without paint, harpists without string, sharks without teeth, sinners without sin.

Catching Salvatore Favazza, executive secretary of the Gloucester Fisheries Commission, in a philosophical mood a couple of days ago, I thought I might get from him some support for my perhaps overly optimistic view that over-fishing won't remain much of a problem after we've finished doctoring the available supply with mercury or whatever other chemical blessings are within our grasp.

Sam, however, is not the man to be panicked. He prefers to cross his bridges of disaster one by one. So he maintains that the most real and present of the various calamities at hand is the adamant refusal of Mr. and Mrs. Haddock to reproduce themselves at a cooperative rate.

Is it possible, I wondered, that old melanogrammus aeglefinus could go the way of the Atlantic halibut, the sperm whale and the passenger pigeon — so overkilled he might not be able to muster the troops for a comeback? We both hoped not. At the least (and then only with the tenderest of international mollycoddling) it will be years, Sam thinks, before haddock will again be king, if ever.

Contrarily, herring looks good to the executive secretary. As for shrimp, who knows? We have the boats, the know-how and the overseas market and transport, but the little wigglies are a temperamental lot, and they just must have cold water. A bit of a warming trend, certain subtle changes in the ocean and the atmosphere brought about by the devil's mark of man, and pfft — no more shrimp.

Pollock, the undiscussable, we didn't discuss. Whiting, yes. An offshore potential for the bigger boats. The foreign fleets have been blitzing whiting, but the locals have kept inshore after them, and they're getting scarce on the coast. Ocean quahog, a possibility. Fishfurters, unspeakable, hence unspoken of.

What about '71 — not war, inflation, pollution, poverty, pot, pornography and plague — but fishing?

It's going to be, in Sam's opinion, a hard year — in spite of the fact that the ex-vessel domestic landing at Gloucester for 1970 will prove out to over eight million bucks, the highest since around 1953, which is surprisingly good, even allowing for inflation.

This year Gloucester will get the full whack from the haddock crisis, and another good belt for good measure from the Argentine whiting imports. And,

he sighed, shrimp shows definite signs of weakness.

Herring, only herring, holds out some hope for the New Year. Herring is good, and it could get better. After all, they actually eat herring in Europe.

The way Favazza sees it, world fisheries conservation depends absolutely on international cooperation, which means national catch quotas, which means spreading the butter over the whole loaf. Evening out the hills and valleys of fishing under quotas can't be done without federal legislation permitting fishermen and processors to have production and marketing agreements.

Cooperatives? The only answer. Unlimited competition for limited resources has brought us where we are.

As one Shakespearean fisherman remarked to the other:

"Master, I marvel how the fishes live in the sea."

To which the reply: "Why, as men do aland; the great ones eat up the little ones."

And their mercury with them, one might add. An unpleasant subject to be sure, which is probably why we never got back, Sam and me, to how much of the stuff is in the

sea, and in we and thee.

January 2, 1971

Swordfish were being condemned at the time on account of possibly toxic levels of mercury, an early spectre of ocean pollution. A far-seeing insurance man from a fishing family, the late Sam Favazza pioneered in establishing the Gloucester Fisheries Commission.

20. GOD DAM. I'M THROUGH WITH FISHIN' —⚓—

"I DON' WANNA MILLION DOLLARS. I don' wanna thousand dollars. I'll take a hunnert dollars for her. Gimme fifty. God dam. I'm through with fishin'. I don' wan no more part of her. Gimme a dollar and take her off my hands before they sink her."

Captain Joseph Palazola of Middle Street drove the proposition home by spitting vigorously off the end of Seven Seas Wharf and glaring at his beloved *Rosie & Gracie*, laying placidly alongside the Gloucester House. She is the most decrepit and historic dragger in the Gloucester fleet, which is going some.

Nigger Joe, as he has been known on the waterfront for his swarthy features since less racially sensitive days, is 69 and of Sicilian stock though he looks like a leathered old Cherokee chief. He has lived in and fished out of Gloucester for 55 years,

and he has had it. This is the end of the line. "T'hell with it. I'm through."

Rosie & Gracie is 54 years old and has been fishing out of here since the 30s, when Joe's late brother-in-law Phil Filetto brought her up from the New Jersey coast where she is alleged to have been rebuilt. Joe bought her from Phil, he thinks it was 1943, for something like $30,000.

Let the record show that *Rosie* was built in 1917 at Neponset as a wooden submarine chaser for the United States Navy shortly after we entered World War I. She is the next to the last of her noble line in Gloucester, and like the disgusted old fisherman who coaxed her tired planks through our waters seining and dragging for the past 28 years, she also has had it.

This is, or appears to be, the end of the line for the dowager

Joe Palazola

Rosie & Gracie, *Harbor Cove*

of the Gloucester fleet. Unless somebody turns up in the next few days to relieve Joe finally and conclusively of all responsibility for her, the US Army Engineers has agreed to do so by towing *Rosie & Gracie* out to the deep water, opening her seacocks and giving her the deep six. If this mercy killing is permitted, then Sam Nicastro's *Serafina N.* will be the lone survivor of Gloucester's once great fleet of converted sub-chasers, 18 or 20 of them in the 30's.

Captain Palazola has seen the handwriting on the pilothouse wall for a long time, but the sentence was completed only a little over three weeks ago. They were dragging not far off-

shore, the skipper, his son Jerry, who has been with him for 26 years, and a crewman. "Well, we lost oil pressure. We dunno what it was. We come in ourselves OK. Took out an tied up an took off the soundin machine an nets an wire an we ain't been out since.

"I says this is it. I'm sick o' the god dam boat. I dunno what's wrong with the engine. Who knows? Mebbe it's nothin. Mebbe it's the pump, or the spray nozzles. Mebbe it's the main bearins. Who knows? Mebbe it's somethin else. Mebbe you can fix it for fifty dollars, hunnert dollars, two hunnert dollars. Who knows?"

He outspread his callused

hands in eloquent resignation.

"It's a good engine, a GM 310 I think. Phil had an old Atlas 200 in her, an after six, seven years I put the GM in. Runs good. Got a good Lister charger below. Good deck winch . . . pretty good . . . you know, works pretty good. Look at them . . . good gallows. Good block up there. She needs a new set o' batteries . . . they ain't so hot.

"She don' leak much. Look there . . . every 25 minutes mebbe she pump five, six gallon. I make some money off her over the years. Summers, five, six thousand . . . but this year, lousy . . . no fish at all."

Leo Linquata joined us. He wants to get *Rosie & Gracie* out of there before she takes the plunge alongside his wharf.

"I'll tell you one thing about her," observed Leo. "She's the only subchaser I ever saw with a keelson in her. It must be this thick . . . and she's the only one didn't twist. They were so limber, you know, why in a seaway they'd twist and squirm around like they was sponge rubber. But not this one."

I suggested to Leo that I might take her and run her up on Niles Beach and make a restaurant out of her and give him and Mike and their Gloucester House a little friendly competition.

"Go ahead," he smiled, as if he knew something he thought I didn't.

"They tole me at the Railways they wouldn't haul her even for cash," sighed Joe. "So I go to Boston today. I go to one office, an they send me to another, an then somewheres else, I don' know where, an then I go to the Engineers an they say they have a man down in coupla weeks to take her out an sink her."

He glared at me sadly.

"So you got two weeks to find someone to take her. I don' care what they give me. I don' care if I get nothin. I just wanna get her off my hands. Linsky won' even take her for junk

"I'll do my best," said I, taking my leave.

"You find someone wants the boat," Captain Palazola called after me, "you tell em I'm down Gloucester Grocery most o' the day."

Harry Cusick, manager of the Gloucester Marine Railways, confirmed that their ways and the *Rosie* had parted for-

ever.

"No, never again," he admitted. "I'm scared of her. She might die right there on the cradle, and then where would we be? They've been sleeping in the pilothouse because you can see daylight through the focsle plankings , and they didn't use the fish hold . . . kept the catch in boxes on deck."

I had to concede that I didn't think *Rosie & Gracie* would ever pass for a hospital ship.

"You know, a few years ago we hauled her," mused Harry, "and we found two whole planks missing below the waterline. All that kept her afloat was where the inside sheathing had been caulked and cemented around the hole. Nope, I wouldn't haul her for anything."

They have a history, these old subchasers. Larry McEwen, now retired as one of Gloucester's first-rate vessel owners, recalls that there were none in our fishing fleet when he came here in 1921, so they presumably were still under Navy mothballs then.

Larry doesn't recollect their armament but remembers that yachtsman Alexander (Sandy) Moffat of Manchester as a naval officer took a fleet of them across

in the First War (Captain Palazola had heard somewhere that
Rosie & Gracie "had been to the
Old Country" — seen service in
the Mediterranean).

They were built long and
incredibly narrow — 104 feet
stem to stern, according to the
records, on a slim 14-foot beam,
drawing only seven feet. Fast as
hell, Larry remembers, with three
big gasoline engines side by side
turning triple screws. Think of it.

The subchasers began
showing up in Gloucester in the
late 20's. Captain Lem Firth had
one for a while. Most were converted to seining, being short on
deck room for dragging. And so
narrow in the hold, to tell the
truth, that you couldn't get a
trip of mackerel unless you
packed 'em the long way, fore
and aft, head to tail.

If they were fast enough to
depth-charge German U-boats,
the subchasers must have the
stuff to run down the rumrunners . . . or so Uncle Sam thought,
and a small flotilla was loaned
by the Coast Guard to the Prohibition Bureau in the early 20's.

But the sauce for the goose
was as good for the gander, and
the rummies commenced to ac-
quire surplus subchasers on their

own account, which rather
evened things up until the
Coolidge administration got the
bright idea of turning some old
destroyers over to the Coasties.

So there's the story of *Rosie
& Gracie* and Captain Joe Palazola. And if somebody with an
overdose of ambition and imagination doesn't show up within
about l0 days and rescue her, the
ancient lady will join the shades
of her sisters in whatever happy
harbor the ghost fleets of the
subchasers lie at anchor.

If her Lochinvar doesn't
come along, and if she does have
to take the plunge (as perhaps she
should, after all), then why not
in a gurgle of glory, to the sound
of taps wafted across the mother
waters, and a champagne toast
by all hands and admirers of the
old subchasers that never die
but just fade, fade away?

II

THREE AND A HALF WEEKS LATER...

WHEN THOSE FIFTY PLUGS OF DY-
namite went off just below her
waterline, I guess she knew she'd
taken her last fish, all right —
the kind they called a torpedo
when she was a subchaser in
World War I.

As soft as an overripe wa-

termelon, *Rosie & Gracie* was
towed out to the deep water the
end of August by the Army Engineers. There, over a 22-fathom
hump on the bottom, they scuttled her. Captain Palazola did-
n't have the heart to make the
trip himself.

It was a simple case of eu-
thanasia. Remember Bill
Mauldin's wartime cartoon of
the grizzled cavalry topkick
standing beside his crippled jeep,
covering his eyes from the pain
of it, about to shoot it through
the hood with his forty-five?
That's why the skipper stayed
ashore that last trip. He could-
n't pull the trigger.

So here was the *Rosie &
Gracie*, very nearly the oldest
and sure as hell the most decrepit vessel in the Gloucester
fleet, the next to the last (to the
Serafina N.) of the famous converted subchasers, hobbling veteran of that first war to save
democracy from Deutschland
uber Alles . . . here she was, worn
out and unwanted, being
dragged out Gloucester Harbor
to be scuttled by the nation she
had served so well . . . out past a
giant German factory ship loaded
to her poops with these frozen
fish that are tightening the full

nelson of subsidized competition on *Rosie* and all her sisters.

Literally, of course, Captain Palazola was the one to deliver the death decree on his beloved companion of 28 years. But her age and condition represented the inevitable geriatric fate of all the Gloucester fleet. No yard would haul her, she was so rotten, and he could not even give her away. She worked almost to the end, but the good days of abundance on the fished-out grounds were over. And indeed her dark-faced old skipper at 69 was all fished out himself, sick of it, tired and ready to quit the sea.

Old vessels, old gear, old methods and old men . . . that's Gloucester today. And her fleet, what's left of it, wears the black mark of fate. The new boats aren't being built, and the old ones are going one by one — scuttled or torpedoed, by foe or by friend.

For years my old pal, Captain Bill Sibley of the small dragger *Peggybell* (and vice chairman of the Gloucester Fisheries Commission) has fumed that the government is deliberately destroying the domestic ground-fishing industry, and I've scoffed

The Gloucester fleet of wooden subchasers converted to seining, soon after World War II. Note seineboats with nets, and crow's nests for spotting schools of mackerel.

at his persecution complex.

Then I saw an unnamed federal official quoted in the July issue of the *National Fisherman* as stating with regard to foreign competition:

"We should buy our fish from other countries that have the means to supply the demand and write off our crummy little (New England) system. Only the strong fisheries in the U.S. should be allowed to survive, like tuna, shrimp and, up to now, lobstering. What will remain is the best."

So maybe Sib was right, the Feds have written off with a vengeance what one so sneeringly dismisses as "our crummy little system," the same system that President John Adams, the strongest admirer they ever had, said 190 years ago produced "the boldest men alive."

Yes, the oldest continuously producing industry in the Western Hemisphere is located here in Gloucester, Massachusetts — the one industry on which the nation was founded — and it struggles along yet, against the insults and scuttlings of small men, without a single, sincere, consistent, powerful, fighting advocate anywhere that I can see on the ladder of government from City Hall to the White House.

Your cussed independent fishermen have never been a political force, and they never will be. They're too obstinate and too thickheaded to get together, and they don't know their own interests, and they don't have any leadership. But what makes my blood boil is the cynical duplicity with which they have been exploited by the very government that should be protecting them from the entrepreneurs of their industry and from the subsidized ravages of other fishing nations.

After generations of neglecting the fishermen in favor of the farmers and other economic groups, Washington tosses the starved remains to the wolves of overseas competition (in many cases already fattened on the American dollar). And when Canada and Denmark and Norway and Germany and Poland and Russia and Japan have about finished them off, some chubby chair warmer has the unbelievable gall to peer over his pile of sextuplet reports and coldly order the offending skeleton to be removed from his view.

Write them off, shrugs the civil servant. Let the fit survive, sniffles he, from his air-conditioned office.

Mayhap he's right, this expert, for all I know. But the programmed ruthlessness of the technocrat is not for me. The seeds of my ancestors are in my loins, as Whitman would say, and they are the roots of the future. I would not bury Gramps before his time has come, merely because he's a leetle past his prime.

No, I would not tear that tattered codfish down, for long has it hung on high, up there in the House of Representatives of the Great and General Court of the Commonwealth of Massachusetts — the gilt symbol, as good as gold, of the proud pursuit that started it all here on the shores of the New World, across the harbor from my window.

And so what do you think now of that Neville Chamberlain of ours who is so anxious to write off our crummy little fishery and hand it to the grinning Krauts, triumphant at last, after two world wars, over a subchaser named *Rosie & Gracie?*

August 14 and
September 18, 1971

21. IF NOT BETTER, NEXT YEAR WILL BE DIFFERENT ～

APOLLO 8 IS HALF WAY HOME AS I write. It will have glided the rest of the distance from the moon by the time you read this, and surely splashed down safe with its three earthmen.

It is the imponderable finale of a year of shock, irony and foreboding, of degradation and sublimation for the human race, a year of anguish and of anger, of no turning-back, ending spectacularly, as it has run its course, on the grand scale.

Nothing small about 1968 . . . a year of grand aspiration . . .and of poignant frustration . . . a year of awful tragedy . . . and of the surging, vernal power of youth . . . a year with hate, fear, love, courage scrawled large across it . . . a year of mass homicide, and suicide . . . and a year of hope tenuous as a thread.

A year so at odds with itself as a unit of evolution that its last legacy is a rocket called Saturn thrusting a capsule called Apollo out through the pollution of the planet into the sterility of space, a bullet shot through the outhouse roof . . . a mission to transplant life, and therefore death, to a place where there is neither.

Are we preparing now to poison the universe with people? Are we venturing, like Icarus of mythology, so near to the sun that the god Apollo, whose name we have taken, will in his wisdom melt the wax of our wings?

Is this the last trip or the first? Are we leaping into a great new world — this playing catch with the moon — or are we being pushed into the abyss by, let's say, something as ridiculous as our sex drive?

Well, who can help but be utterly awed by the moon shot?

Yet I think I would just as soon, if you don't mind, hear His Holiness the Pope say something about birth control that was at least remotely related to the 20th century.

And if I had my way, I'd elect to assign some of the men and taxes that are being shot to hell or heaven from Vietnam and Cape Kennedy to such earthbound enterprises as exploring the black side of this planet, and orbiting the inner reaches of the protoplasm to know some more about how it lives and why it dies, and probing the galaxies of cells we call people in the hope of discovering why they are so out of tune with the music of the spheres.

What I started out to observe was that all things have a way of coming home at last, like Apollo 8 at 25,000 miles an hour.

Charles A. Lindbergh

Centennial Johnson in mid-Atlantic

who checked out every nut, bolt and inch of wire in his air flivver. And then *"We"* took off on a drag race against time and 3500 miles of ocean.

A few days after Lindy sputtered in out of the fog and touched down at Le Bourget airfield, a Boston reporter came down to Gloucester to see what old Captain Alfred Johnson thought of it all. Centennial was full of admiration. "They called Lindy the Flying Fool," said he. "But me, they called me a damn fool — and they were right. I was a harumscarum sort of feller then and didn't have a grain o' sense in my head."

True enough. His waterfront cronies dared him to try, and like a fool he did. But Johnson spent two years preparing for that day in June of 1876 when he sailed out of Gloucester in his 16-foot banks dory christened in honor of the centennial of American independence.

Centennial Johnson, with faith in his craft and himself, made it in that wooden "capsule," propelled by wind, tide, skill and will at an average speed of three knots. He landed on the coast of Wales 64 days later, the first man in all time to cross the

created no less of a sensation in May of 1927, a mere 41-minus years ago, when he flew across the Atlantic from New York to Paris in 33 hours. The speed of Lindy's *Spirit of St. Louis* was not much better than a hundred miles an hour. I remember waving from a fifth-story window above Beacon Street when he paraded triumphantly through Boston. Fantastic. No back-up, no Mission Control — just a kid

North Atlantic Ocean alone that we have any record of.

His epic, dory included, cost him $200 he saved from fishing.

The boat is down at the Cape Ann Historical, where it belongs. Perhaps it deserves some day to be dry-docked alongside of the *Spirit of St. Louis* and Apollo 8 at the Smithsonian Museum in Washington, because Centennial Johnson is a man for all time too.

Magellan, Columbus, Smith, Champlain, Johnson, Slocum, Blackburn, Chichester, Shepard, Borman, Lovell, Anders . . . a great company of men who dared to cross their own particular horizons.

Man's explorations have a way of returning to their origins. This bitter cold, star-punched night after Christmas, I gaze up at that brilliant half-moon, hanging there above my dark-sided earth.

Somewhere between here and there, three of my flesh and blood, my brothers, are drifting back, in the pull of home, in the grip of eternity.

I guess I'll stick around for another year at that.

December 27, 1968

On the Wind

22. HOW OLD SOUNDS STICK IN THE EARS ⟨⟩

STRANGE HOW SOME OLD SOUNDS stick in the memory of the ears. When I was a lad we spent a few weeks each summer in my grandmother's cottage at Riverview, and every dawn I awoke (I can hear it now, just as clear) to the engines of the draggers laboring through Squam River for the Bay, and the lobster boats.

Most of the vessels then had those slow-turning Wolverine and Atlas diesels. The still air before sunrise throbbed to the deep bass of their CHUG a da CHUG a da CHUG a da . . . receding as they passed by to round the bar below Thurston's Point, the swish of the wake slapping up along the flats.

And then the next, growing louder as the first died out, coming up along by Rust Island, and the next — a mean-dering file of ponderous sea elephants, almost trunk to tail.

Some days when it was thick I would leap from bed to window, straining through the fog for a glimpse, but nothing was to be seen beyond a shrouded maple, dripping wet. Only the sound from down below somewhere, muffled, dogged . . . CHUG a da CHUG a da CHUG a da . . .

How could they ever navigate that corkscrew of a channel, bow scarcely visible from the pilot house? No radar or depth sounder then. Once in a while they didn't, and when the fog scaled up by mid-morning, there they'd be half out of water on the sand bar, with nothing much to do but dig clams, play cards, mug up and wait for the tide to come.

Or a lobsterman going by nursing along his old Lath-rop . . . putt putt putt putt (silence while the flywheel spins) putt putt (silence) putt (silence) putt putt putt (silence) putt . . . and off down the river.

The sounds of Cape Ann . . . some are gone forever, like the hesitant stutter of the make-and break-engine, except where some antique boat buff like Bill Lee has nursed a Lawley launch back to life at East Gloucester.

Gone is the fire whistle at the electric company, music to us in proportion to our distance from it — exciting, foreboding, full of disaster in the night. Before it finally ran out of steam, the old tooter had taken the steam out of a thousand torrid love scenes on the silver screen of the North Shore Theater across the street with 8-5-3 blasts (count 'em!) to an alarm on Magnolia Avenue or wherever. Wow! The ears still ring.*

We have the railroad yet, though we nearly lost it. Coming into the Depot the clanking steam locomotives of olden times gave forth full-throated, wailing shrieks of melancholy that loomed and echoed down the harbor from shore to shore. Now the Buddliners honk on oversized tricycle horns, but the sound seems to mean the same as ever, especially from afar — a comforting reminder that Cape Ann, for all its queer ways, is still tolerated by the rest of mankind.

And the grinding and clanking of the great black gears raising the railroad bridge at Dunfudgin . . . the lofty mast of your boat passes under and you glance up nervously and pray that this infernal machine, this monstrous guillotine, this towering mandible of Beelzebub won't take a fancy to the passer-through and descend for a taste.

Gone is the symphony of clattering, tinkering, banging, blasting, grinding, wheezing voices of the quarries, but still pounding in our heads the dogmatic, cacophonic, skull-shattering anvil chorus of the Cape Ann Tool Works.**

Yet the sounds that stick in the ears for life are not the noisy ones, the bullies, but the sounds of the sea where it meets the coast and the sea works of man, carried from off a way on the wind or through the placid air or inside the fog.

Swell, surf, surge, combing, breaking, crashing, lapping, roiling, whispering, roaring . . . gull's hoarse cry, scream of tern. And man's sounds at sea . . . the bells of the Breakwater*** . . . gentle clanger off Norman's Woe . . . the sad, oh so sad, resigned dirge of the whistler, Mother Ann's Cow, sobbing on the back of an easterly . . . distant hooting diaphones of Bakers and Thacher's, and the Isles of Shoals a way way off . . .

The boy T.S. Eliot summered on Eastern Point and soaked up sounds that stuck in his ears to emerge forty years later in "The Dry Salvages":

. . . The sea howl
And the sea yelp, are different voices
Often together heard, the whine in the rigging,
The menace and caress of wave that breaks on water,
The distant rote in the granite teeth,
And the wailing warning from the approaching headland
Are all sea voices, and the heaving groaner
Rounded homewards, and the seagull:
And under the oppression of the silent fog
The tolling bell. . .

Who has ever so captured the menace and caress of Cape Ann and its sea but Tom Eliot, expatriate to England, forever haunted by the summer sounds of his childhood?

January 22, 1968

---

* Every house had a card posted in the kitchen with the alarm box numbers and locations; half the town counted the whistles, jumped in the car, and got to the scene ahead of the apparatus.

** Since gone too.

*** The two steeple-sized fog bells at the Eastern Point Lighthouse and the end of Dog Bar Breakwater were replaced forever the following year, in April 1969.

23. A LITTLE COW GOES A LONG WAY

Emmeline
Has not been seen
For more than a week.
She slipped between
The two tall trees at the end
of the green ...
We all went after her.
"Emmeline!"

EVEN IF GREAT-GRANDFATHER Garland's cow was named Emmeline, she did not inspire A.A. Milne's lines from "When We Were Very Young," which do not concern a cow anyway.

Dr. Joseph followed his brother, Deacon George, down from Hampton, N.H., in 1841 and taught school three winters at Freshwater Cove to earn his way through college and medical school before he started the practice of medicine in Gloucester in 1849.

They dynamited his house on Pleasant Street to stop the Great Fire of 1864 from spreading north. Later he removed home and office to Dale Avenue and long after he died in 1902 at 80, they tore that down for the new post office.

The white-bearded old physician owned a homestead out on Eastern Avenue, south of the Nugent Stretch, above Joppa in what they once called The Farms. The house stands yet, with its old fashioned veranda, still known to the natives as the Garland place.

Great-Grandpa lived on the farm for a few years before he moved to Dale Avenue. One afternoon in the summer of 1882, the year after he retired from two terms as the city's fifth mayor — it was along around the end of August, Thursday the 24th to be exact — his hired man went out as usual to milk the cow, but Bossie or Emmeline or what-

Great-grandpa

ever was nowhere to be found.

Well — No cow, no milk. No milk, no cream. No cream no butter for the bread. What a nuisance.

So Dr. Garland stopped by the office of the *Cape Ann Weekly Advertiser* and put in a notice that his cow was missing from Cape Pond pasture, with a good clinical description of the animal, and advised that the finder would be promptly rewarded upon her return.

Another week went by, and still no Emmeline, so on the eighth of September he dug down and posted a $20 reward.

One more milkless, creamless and butterless week and Dr. Garland, universally beloved and ordinarily the most benign man on Cape Ann, was so thoroughly aroused and by now convinced that he had been victimized, that he hied himself down to the City Marshal.

For the next three weeks in a row there appeared in the *Advertiser* the following notice, having all the earmarks of a medical record, and surely the

Great-grandpa's cow

most particular description of a bovine in the history of Essex County and possibly America.

$100 REWARD! COW STOLEN

JERSEY COW, nine years or older, good size, thin flesh, pale red or fawn color, patches of white on shoulders, legs and brisket; udder and belly white; face and neck slightly dark; dark on lower sides; muzzle dark, with light circles; eyes full, with light circles; horns rather long and white, but darker near head and tips; dark spots on horns near head, where rope had worn creases, horns set upwards and forwards, one turning inwards and dropping a little, brass knob on each horn; rump straight, with spot bare of hair near

backbone; tail long and slender; udder large, deepest behind; back teats lowest and shortest; hoofs long, dewclaws very large; somewhat lame in forward feet; missed from Cape Pond pasture, Gloucester and Rockport, since Aug. 24th.

$20 reward will be paid for the recovery of cow, and $100 reward for recovery of cow and conviction of thief.

Joseph A. Moore,
City Marshal

Still no cow.

Now by all accounts, my great-grandfather was not a man given to snap judgments. But he appears to have missed the diagnosis in this case, for on the following fateful Friday the 13th of October it was closed thus in the news columns of the *Advertiser*:

"Dr. Garland's cow, which had been missing for several weeks and was supposed to have been stolen from Cape Pond Pasture, was found by two little girls Friday, tightly wedged between two trees in the pasture, starved to death."

January 27, 1968

24. THANKSGIVING ON THE INSTALLMENT PLAN ~—

THE EARLY DAYS OF PROHIBITION, *before the Mob muscled in, were for ordinarily more or less law-abiding seafaring men and their shoreside pals full of excitement and easy money (sort of) evocative of smuggling and shades of Sherwood Forest. The inane Eighteenth Amendment to the US Constitution no less, outlawing the manufacture and sale of alcoholic beverages in America, couldn't have been more perfectly designed to be honored in the breach, and so it was, from one side of the bar to the other.*

How better to hide a load of booze than under a load of fish? From the day the Volstead Act was passed in 1919 Cape Ann, with all its coves and concealments and fisherman's foolhardihood was a major hotbed of joyous cops-and-robberhood on the Atlantic seaboard.

The Robin Hood of these merry men was the daring and charismatic Bill McCoy, skipper-owner of the handsome Glouces-ter fishing schooner Arethusa *which he bought and renamed* Tomoka *and made flagship of the Rum Row fleet of suppliers that hung around on the edge of the twelve-mile limit. Though he en-titled his autobiography "The Real McCoy" in exaltation of the qual-ity of his stock in trade, the phrase was first applied in Scotland to the true chief of the Mackay clan and is said to have been altered in America to fit Kid McCoy, the legendary world welterweight champion of 100 years ago. Bill McCoy was a real golfer too, play-ing Bass Rocks between business trips on the high seas.*

A thousand stories lie buried in the pages of the Times *of the Rip-Roaring Twenties, and here are a few.*

THE DAWN WAS RAW THIS MONDAY before Thanksgiving one year in the Roaring Twenties, and the two Gloucestermen and their "banker" buttoned jackets against the wind as their open 30-footer headed out the Harbor and around the Breakwater.

Mike and Long Haul Paul were fishermen. The Banker was from up the line, and he had $3,500 in his pocket. Desti-nation was somewhere 40 miles to the eastward, where they were to rendezvous with a foreign supply ship and exchange the long green for a load of booze.

In short, they were rum-runners. But as this was before the rackets had shot all the laughs out of Prohibition, and the good guys weren't all on the side of the law, Mike and Long Haul Paul had thoughtfully brought along a turkey and the fixings and a steak to brace up Thanksgiving

Bill McCoy mans a Lewis machine gun aboard the former Gloucester fishing schooner Arethusa.

for the boys on the big boat.

When the motorboat reached the supposed rendezvous area, however, the ocean was empty. They cruised around for a while, concluded with disappointment and some profanity that they had been stood up for reasons unknown, and struck back for Cape Ann.

They had to buck a freshening northwest wind and rising seas. Spray flew, and they took green water over the bow. The boat bounced and pounded, and the working of the planks started a leak. Hour after hour they fought on, when a sudden

dousing killed the engine, and nothing would revive it. Long Haul Paul labored at the pump, Mike with a five-gallon alky can. The Banker was deathly seasick and no use; they stowed him on a bunk in the cuddy.

The norwester swept over them all night. Trying to keep warm, they rolled the Banker onto the floor, ripped up the bunks and fed them into the rusty stove. It gave enough heat to barely singe the turkey and steak.

All the next day, Tuesday, they drifted before the offshore gale, past Cape Cod, the last of the land a line on the horizon. They had brought no fresh water, but the fishermen succeeded in condensing a few spoonfuls from a pan of seawater on the stove.

The fire kept going out, and inevitably their last match with it. Wet and shivering cold, they cast about for some kind of substitute. They had long since used up all the paper on board when an ironic inspiration took hold of them.

Seasickness and exhaustion by now had driven the Banker to the edge of delirium, and at times when he roused from his stupor they had to restrain him. It occurred to the rummies to relieve him of his bankroll a bill at a time. Mike would dip a C-note in gasoline, which Long Haul Paul would ignite with a spark from the battery and thrust into the stove.

Thus, on the installment plan, they coaxed and recoaxed the fire back to life.

At dusk Wednesday a three-masted schooner hove into view, bearing right for them. Frantically the two fishermen pulled off their jackets. They soaked them in gasoline and set them afire with battery sparks.

They were sure they were seen, for no sooner did these torches flare up than the schooner came sharply about and sailed away.

During the night the leak increased to a line of geysers. The boat was falling apart underneath them. The ceaseless pounding had done its work; she was splitting open like a rotten melon.

Mike found a length of rope, and after many tries he and Long Haul Paul submerged one end, fished it up around the other side amidships and tied the ends across the cockpit. They twisted this taut with a stock of wood, and the planks closed somewhat.

Thursday was Thanksgiving, but the dinner was long gone. Around noon a knockabout schooner beat past them on the way into market, only a quarter mile off, but their shouts went unheard. They huddled under the deck, bailing, feeding Treasury notes and splinters into the stove, forcing a few drops of condensed water between the teeth of the almost unconscious Banker, sticking their heads out to search the empty tossing ocean.

And so it went all night,

all day Friday, all Friday night. The Banker would stir and mumble and lapse again, blue with the cold. The wind blew on and on, driving them out to sea.

Some time Saturday a beam trawler slogged by, two miles off, and disappeared to the westward with the last of their hopes. The day and the night dragged on. They felt death.

Sunday morning was the seventh day. The end must be near.

Very weakly Mike raised his head above the gunwale. Only half a mile away, a dragger lurched in the trough, setting out the net. He could hear the clatter of the winch.

The two rumrunners fell to their knees and prayed, then waved their arms and croaked, hoarsely.

Figures moved at the dragger's rail. The winch reversed and the net came in. Already she was wallowing towards them.

The Banker lay motionless. They kicked him, and he stirred slightly. Their rescuers, alongside now, lowered a sling. The Gloucestermen fastened the Banker in, and he was hoisted aboard. Then they dragged themselves up the rope ladder and were pulled over the rail.

They were on the outer edge of Georges Bank, 160 miles from Cape Ann.

In two more days the Banker was in the hospital, and Mike and Long Haul Paul were back in Gloucester, where they told the newspapers how they had spent Thanksgiving on the installment plan.

November 24, 1967

Out of consideration for the sensibilities of this trio of everybody's-doing-it felons of long ago, I refrained from using their real names. The evening the column appeared the lone survivor phoned me indignantly and wanted to know why I hadn't.

25. DRY RUN AT MANCHESTER-BY-THE-SEA, SEE? ⎯⚬⎯

THIS HERE IS A REAL PLUSH SUMmer mansion in Manchester — which the hoity-toities call Manchester-by-the-Sea, see, so the visitin' swells won't mix it up with Manchester-by-the-Mills — on Boardman Avenue, and it belongs to Mister Lester Leland Esquire of Beacon Street in the Back Bay of Boston, a very important man indeed in rubber who happens to be doin' the European circuit right now, which explains why there ain't none of the family around.

So it's the fourteenth of March, which is the day before the Ides of March, whatever the hell that is, in the year of nineteen hunnert and twenty-one.

In other words, the Bad Old Days (hot cha) of what they called the Noble Experiment are just about gettin' up steam. This here Mister Leland's servants are holdin' down the joint

under the ever watchful orbs of the housekeeper, and there's a whole gang of workmen, see, tramplin' the shrubbery, poundin' holes in the roof, racin' around paperin' the woodwork, spillin' paint on the Orientals et cetera.

Up the private driveway slides this big black sedan, and bringin' up the rear a panel truck. They screech to a very polite stop, see, skitterin' gravel all over the grass, and three very businesslike lookin' gents climb out of the sedan, march up to the front door hup, hup, hup, and the front man gives the button a jab with a manicured forefinger.

Comes the butler. Sir? sez he.

The boss guy, very neat in his pin-striped serge, identifies himself as Mister William J. McCarthy, Supervisor of Prohibition Enforcement in New Eng-

land, and these are my men, see, and he quick-flashes a badge and a John Doe warrant, and lemme talk to the housekeeper.

Up she comes on the double. What's this? she wants to know.

They flash their stuff at her, and she backs away, and then like they know just where they're goin' the three of 'em waltz right across the carpets, past the lines of flunkies and workmen watchin' with their mouths hangin' open and down the cellar stairs, the lady in charge trottin' along behind, see.

Right to the door of the wine cellar. Where's the key, lady? Oh, dearie me, I don't have it, Mister Leland must have taken it to Europe with him.

Well that's all right, sez the Chief, and he sends one of the boys hot-footin' it out to the sedan. He's back in a jiffy with a bag full of very interestin' tools like you never saw in the hardware store, and in another jiff the door's open, and there it all is.

Aha, exclaims the Chief, rubbin' his hands, these are the beauties now. They sure look natural, those labels, now don't they boys? Let's hustle along.

And he trots up to the front door, gives the truck the high sign, see, which they bring right up to the steps and two characters jump out of the front and four more hop out of the back. This way men, orders the Chief, and they two-step in betwixt the rows of spectators, peelin' off their jackets and down the stairs to the wine cellar. Lively now and pile all this stuff in the truck, but don't break nothin', see.

And boy don't the cases and the bottles start movin', and the finest kind of stuff, like the bucket brigade at the fire, and when the housekeeper starts to put up a squawk the Chief throws her a hard look and growls she better not interfere with the process of the law.

So the servants and the painters and all are standin' around takin' all this in, see, watchin' the hootch bein' passed up to the truck, and a couple of the carpenters commence to mumble and make noises like maybe this don't look to them like it's entirely on the up and up, know what I mean.

Well, it's right then that some of the Chief's deputies while they're workin' along there handin' the booze along get to talkin' kinda loud about the time on the raid they had to use their revolvers, and the mutterin' on the sidelines stops like somebody shot out the light.

In another coupla minutes the wine cellar is bare as Mother Hubbard's cupboard, and on with their jackets, and pack up their tools, and out past the servants and the guys. Pardon the inconvenience, sez the Chief, and he tips his lid politely and bows to the housekeeper, and then into the sedan and off out the driveway, the panel truck behind, slightly down on its springs.

But the housekeeper smells a rat, maybe nine of them, see, and she calls the Manchester cops and informs them that a very fine appearin' man who said he was Mister McCarthy, the Prohibition Chief, showed up with his deputies, a rather hard lookin' crew, and carried off a hunnert and forty bottles of the best rye whisky and fifty-seven cases of very, very good gin which Mister Leland had stocked in his wine cellar all legal and proper before the Volstead Act was ratified.

When the cops telephone Mister McCarthy in his office in Boston, he is extremely angry and in fact fit to be tied, because this gentle little heist pulled off in his good name at Manchester-by-the-Sea, see, at the bootleg price of fifteen bucks a jug, is worth a cool twelve thousand three hunnert and sixty smackeroos.

March 8, 1988

PS: The hoity-toities prevailed in the end, and today Manchester is officially by-the-Sea. This here Mister Leland was Vice Chairman of US Rubber.

26. OUR KEYSTONE KOPS GAVE KRAZY CHASE

YOU DON'T HAVE TO DELVE VERY deep into the days when the 18th Amendment brought prosperity to Cape Ann to realize that there was a lot more to Prohibition, like the iceberg, than showed on the surface.

Too many folks are around who made a buck off bootleg or got caught to looward of the most asinine law ever passed to be too specific about all the details even 40 odd years later.

"My gaw, gramps! You mean you actually BROKE THE LAW? What! A gun battle with the COAST GUARD! Well, for . . ."

Talk about violence these days . . . there was more of it, land and sea, around Cape Ann between 1920 and 1935 running booze from Rum Row where the liquor ships lay outside the 12-mile limit, and making the stuff, more excitement in those crazy years, I guess, than all the rest of our 350 rolled into one.[*] Some of it was faintly amusing.

Like the night of June 16, 1924, when the Coast Guard got the tip-off and slipped out of the Dolliver's Neck Station in their launch and intercepted a slow-moving runner, the 656C, without any trouble off Baker's Island heading into Beverly.

They grabbed the two guys with 200 cases of alcohol they'd transferred from a three-stick schooner on Rum Row, put a tow line aboard and brought the 656C to anchor in Old House Cove hard by the Station.

The pair went to court and were bailed. That night a young Coasty was assigned to stand guard on the rummy with gun and flashlight.

At about 2 a.m. a boat glided out of the fog alongside of the 656C and before the youthful guard knew what was up his hands were — high, at the point of a pistol. There were two of 'em. They tied and gagged him and put him ashore in a vacant building — right under the snoring noses of the Coast Guard — and then they went back out to start her up and get outa there.

They cranked away and they cranked away, and she wouldn't kick over, and that's the last heard of them. At daybreak a couple of lobstermen pulling their pots heard the young Guardsman's groans and landed and untied him. Nearby they found the 656C that the pirates hadn't been able to start, high and dry on the rocks . . . lacking only five of the 200 cases of alky.

*I'm not sure I'd make that claim today in 1994.

77

Then there was the time Marshal Millard Whidden (we call him the police chief now), Sergeant Cronin, Officer Flaherty and Officer Foley at the wheel were in the Ford that passed for a patrol car in those days, on a scouting expedition . . . in other words, on the prowl for bootleggers.

Turning up Centennial Avenue onto Washington Street, they met up with a brand new two-ton White truck just turning in that looked right suspicious, and the Marshal told Foley to make a U-turn and follow. This was about 9 p.m. on the bitterly cold night of February 6 in 1925, and the roads were a sheet of ice.

This truck had a real heavy load, and when the two men riding in the rear of it saw the cops loop back on them, they motioned to the three up front, and the driver stepped on it.

The truck picked up speed, jounced over the railroad bridge, faster all the time, zipped across Beacon Street, up over the brow and down the steep Centennial slope towards the harbor at full tilt, the carful of Keystone cops right on their tail, the truck waggling back and forth over the ice from curb to curb.

Sergeant Cronin grabbed the riot gun, an automatic, leaned out the window and let go with a warning burst of lead that brought folks running out of their houses into the street.

Somehow or other the truck hit Western Avenue and made the turn without springboarding right into the harbor and the flivver did too, both of 'em on two wheels, rubber screaming, and the truck opened it up across the Cut Bridge, and boy it was really moving going into Essex Avenue.

Cronin emptied his riot gun and threw it down and pulled out his revolver and emptied that too. Roaring across the causeway and heading up Lovett's Hill, the truck was definitely shaking its pursuers.

The sergeant grabbed Flaherty's pistol and cut loose again, this time right at 'em, and just as it looked as if the truck was going to get away after all, a stray shot struck a rear tire, which blew out and that was the end of the chase.

The Model T screeched to a stop, even with the White, and the Marshal leaped into the cab, and handcuffed the driver and the man in the middle together. The third man in front and the two in back took off like deer.

Officer Flaherty, gunless as he was, pointed his forefinger and thumb pistol-fashion at the fleeing figures and roared: "Hands up or I'll shoot!" One stopped in his tracks and was collared. The cops jumped in their tin lizzie and overtook the fourth man way down on the causeway. Number five got away.

The swag? Oh yes . . . 250 gallons of alcohol, 24 bottles of Burgundy, 12 of cognac and 12 of something very exotic called "peppermint glaciale."

December 6, 1968

27. THEY WANTED MORE HAIR OF THE DOG ─⚌─

PROHIBITION HAD ITS LIGHTER side around Cape Ann, there's no denying it, just as war has its laughs . . . and this is the face of the coin you like to keep turned up in memory.

Forgetting about the wholesale lawbreaking, and the moral poison of it, and the murder and mayhem and graft and corruption, and the way it got organized crime started, the Noble Experiment was good for plenty of chuckles, too.

Take this encounter on the shore road going through Beverly Farms. It's the cold afternoon of January 9, 1924, and the cop has just flagged down a heavily laden truck speeding toward Boston.

He draws aside the rear flap and peers in back. Case after case of bottles and carboys.

"Hey driver, whaddya got there anyway?"

"Oh about 300 gallons of the finest kind of cod liver oil that ever came out o' Gloucester, I hope to tell ya."

"Cod liver oil eh? That sounds pretty fishy to me."

"Well, that's what it is, officer, and if ya don't think so, try one on the house."

"Hmmm. This looks like pretty good stuff to me." The policeman rips open a case and withdraws a pint bottle. "Say . . . good color . . . there's a good plant somewheres by the looks of this job."

"You bet. Take a good swig of it , officer, while you're about it."

"Aaarrgghhh. . .!"

And then there's the story about John O'Donnell the old coachman for one of the summer families who lived in the Greenough stable on the road to the Eastern Point Lighthouse.

One black night John thought he heard something around the stone pier at the end of Wharf Beach. So he pulled on his britches and his boots and crossed the road to investigate.

Sure enough, a launch was alongside the landing, and some guys were busy making a transfer of bottled goods.

"Hi thire, you fillas, wat th' hill's going' on thire?"

John was a big Irishman with a high piping voice and you could hear him all the way to East Gloucester Square.

One of the figures broke away from the rest, came running up to John and tucked a pistol in his ribs.

"Shaddup, shaddup," he hissed, "and if yer know what's good fer yer, old man, get t'hell outa here and go back to beddy-by."

"Ah, put that ting awye, me bye. This is pry-vit proppity hee-ar, dawn't ye know that? Say wat if oi go back an' put in a jingle t' th' cops now?"

And so on, old John kept at it in that voice of his, enough to raise the dead, and the rummy going SHHHH and trying to quiet him down.

So the only way they could shut John up was to slip him a bottle, and he rolled back to the stable for the rest of his night's sleep, content in the knowledge that he had certainly tried to sound the alarm.

Surely one of the best of the stories about Prohibition in this neck of the woods, classic in its simplicity, concerns the three Federal agents who early in the morning of the eighth of May, 1928, swooped down on a remote shack in the brush a mile from Belcher Street in Essex near the Ipswich line.

The shack was off in back of a piggery. The three, working on a tip, parked their flivver some distance up the dirt road, turned off the ignition and the lights, and moved stealthily in on their prey.

The surprise was complete, and they nabbed five Boston men who had quite an operation going around a rather sophisticated still capable of producing 700 gallons of alcohol a day. The Feds also confiscated 50 gallons of alky and a quantity of fresh mash.

"But how in hell did you ever find us out here in the sticks?" the Improper Bostonians wanted to know.

Well, it seems the agents got their tip from a farmer in the area who noticed his cows had been acting right strange lately.

He'd turn 'em out to pasture every morning, finest kind, but then around noontime they'd come straggling and stumbling back, all bleary and weary and wobbly, and sort of collapse in the yard.

So he followed the herd one day, and d'ye know they went straight through the woods for a bellyful of hair off the dog that bit 'em — a big pile of the giddiest-smellin' mash you ever laid eyes on, out in back of that shack.

January 24, 1969

28. THE LIGHT SIDE O' THEM DAYS ～Ⅲ～

IF EVER A MAN WAS A PRODUCT OF his times it was James Edward Brennan, born in Gloucester in 1898, long since retired when I got to know him early in 1972 after he wrote me such an intriguing reminiscent comment on a column that I dropped by with tape recorder and camera.

Jim was imprisoned by a chronic pulmonary disability most of the time in the apartment he and his wife Rose kept in the Poplar Park elderly housing complex. It was a hard sentence for an exuberant master plumber and steamfitter who bossed a hundred men at the Boston Navy Yard pipe shop in World War II.

Our recording session that 20th of January held me quite spellbound. Jim wheezed and coughed until he could hardly breathe, but what he related was the stuff of living human history. The morning produced four

columns, filled out with my own research, including a reminiscence of Gloucester's own Stuffy McInnis, probably the greatest fielding first baseman of all time, shared with the late Al Flygare and Al Joyce.

A year later, in January 1973, we had another taping session. Jim had been musing about the old days of the steam towboats in Gloucester, and we both wanted to get it down. His lungs were even weaker, but not his mind. It made a concluding posthumous reminiscence. Here they all are in one piece.

Jim Brennan

I

JOHN BRENNAN, JIM'S GRANDFAther, departed Kilkenny, Ireland, for the promised land in 1838. The poison of the shameful anti-Irish Catholic riots of 1834 had infected Boston, so he landed in Philadelphia. "On board of the vessel," as his grandson was told, "around Baltimore, he took what the Irish called the pledge — that is, to drink no more booze." Having a fair education for the times, and though only 21, he landed a job in the ticket office of the early railroad that preceded the Pennsy.

After this John Brennan seems to have gone to sea, and some time around 1850, say, he fell for Catherine Morrissey in Boston where she was "living in" and also teaching school, having fled the famine "to the Boston states" by way of Newfoundland. They married and shifted down to Gloucester, where Jack got a site fishing. They moved into the Irish section around where St. Ann's Church is now, on what was then called Back Street, the westerly extension of Prospect, and an old letter locates them in 1859 in the ancient Garrison House, locale of the legendary Peg Wesson "witch story" related by John A. Babson in his "History of Gloucester"

"You can see the smartness of 'em," says Jim enthusiastically, "because behind the house was a gravel pit they worked to help pay the mortgage." And Grandmother Brennan, between having eight kids, put on "mock trials" in the cellar, sort of informal teaching sessions to drum the ABC's and basics of learning into some of the Irish children in the neighborhood. One of the "culprits" was Sylvester (Sylvie) Whalen who was later mayor, and another was John Flaherty, who with Charles P. Thompson, would be the only superior court judges in Massachusetts ever to come out of Gloucester.

By the outbreak of the Civil War it was going none too good for the Brennans. The third week of February 1862 a fearsome gale swept Georges Bank. Seventy Gloucester vessels were at anchor in the shoal water. When it was over, thirteen were sunk with all hands aboard — 120 men, among them John Brennan, aged 45, gone to the bottom with the other eight in the schooner *Ocean Flower.*

So little care was paid the identity of the thousands of fishermen of Gloucester in those times that in the town death book he was put down as "James Breman," and so he remains today. There were five others like him in the *Ocean Flower . . .*

birthplace, Ireland . . . parentage, unknown . . . cause of death, drowning . . . place of interment, ocean. Five solid pages of them, 120 men, in the death book for February 1862 in the city clerk's vault, their only memorial . . . cause of death, drowning . . . place of interment, ocean . . . vessel after vessel to the count of thirteen.

The *City of Sorrow,* the Boston papers called Gloucester. The flick of one quick storm on Georges left 70 widows and 140 fatherless children.

Dolliver, the owner, foreclosed on the Widow Brennan — "she slammed the door in his face and said you'll get your money on the judgment day" — and she moved with her eight across Cape Ann to Annisquam where she rented the old Haraden homestead on Squam Point, at the river end of Leonard Street.

An owner of yore was Captain Andrew Haraden, he of the grisly retribution. One fine day in April of 1724 he and his crew and his brand new fishing sloop *Squirrel* were taken by the vile pirate John Phillips. They bided their time, and four days later, seizing the tools with which their captor had put them to work on deck, they rose up and regained their vessel. And when Haraden triumphantly returned to Squam, Caesarlike, the severed head of John Phillips stared down from the *Squirrel's* masthead. So says Babson.

Grandma Brennan in her own good way was as dauntless as the doughty captain, and she took in boarders. They were Irish immigrant stonecutters brought to Cape Ann to work the quarries even before the famous Finns. To turn another penny she sold them boots and clothing and such, which she bought from Parsons store up in town. How long she was in the Haraden house her grandson does not know, but the family has a letter she wrote from there, that one of the Harvey boys came around that morning and said President Lincoln had been assassinated.

"Anyway," says Jim, "after the loss of my grandfather the Brennans got leery of the fishing. In later years some of them went, but only just once in a while to make a buck — in Gloucester parlance, one-trip johnnies."

His mother's father was a downeaster, George Jones, who hiked from Jonesport to Portsmouth to enlist aboard the US gunboat *Kearsarge* in 1862. The assumption is that he met up there with Master's Mate John Bickford of East Gloucester, who won the Medal of Honor for heroism during the great naval battle off Cherbourg when she sank the rebel raider *Alabama* on June 19, 1864, because after he was mustered out, Grandpa Jones came to Gloucester and went fishing.

Fishy Jones, people called him, and he lived in a house on Caledonia Place, where Jim's Ma was born, off East Main Street behind the filling station.

One winter trip in Charlie Fred Wonson's schooner, *Starry Flag,* they were running out the outer harbor of Gloucester — this was before the Breakwater — in rough water and a man fell overboard. Fishy Jones jumped in after him and hauled him to the surface and swam him into Niles Beach, and then walked him up through the snow all the way to East Gloucester Square and a warm fire. The fella survived, but Fishy caught pneumonia and died. So Jim lost both grandfathers to the sea.

Neil McEachern and Jim Brennan, Sr., on the vaudeville circuit

II

ONE OF THE EIGHT KIDS GRAND-father Jack left for his widow when he drowned on Georges was Jim's father, whom Jim was named after, and he was a man born for the footlights.

Jim Brennan senior tried this and that, but his first and last love was the stage in a day when vaudeville was king, and Gloucester was hailed as one of the liveliest stops on the New England circuit.

He got started raising money for St. Ann's Roman Catholic Church running benefit minstrel shows in City Hall auditorium, which in those days was regularly leased by the city for theatricals, dances, prize-fights, basketball and so on.

One of his cronies was Bill Kelleher, a tall and distinguished looking guy who years after ran a Gloucester saloon of note. Kelleher entered show business as "Bill" with a team of acrobats and contortionists who billed themselves as the La Barre Brothers. This was 1879, when Kelleher was only 15. The others included Ira (Iry) W. Marshall of Gloucester, a tumbler who later took the stage name Ed La Barre and tended bar for Kelle-her, Billy Burke of Lynn, Brennan, and George Clark of Gloucester, whose brother Bill would become Essex County district attorney.

Gloucester barrister Dick Clark, Clark's nephew and the D.A.'s son, believes that some time afterward, when his show was stranded in South Dakota, his uncle married a local girl and settled down to run a rooming house.

Kelleher hit the trail as advance man and business agent for various road shows such as Sparks Brothers Circus before he returned to his native city and opened his waterfront bar on Porter Street soon after the First War.

Jim recalls hearing that in the 1880's Kelleher, a guy named Curley Roper and William H. Reilly ran a spot down by the Town Landing in Gloucester known as "The Free and Easy" which he credits with being among the first night clubs in the country. One of their stars, he remembers being told, was Mag-gie Kline, who was the Kate Smith of her day, and when she came down from Boston the gang would always get her to sing "Trow 'em down, Mc-Closkey, it is the battle cry!"

This joint was first known as Reilly's Opera House, listed in the city directory as a "Concert saloon" at 18 Commercial Street. Besides running the Central House hotel at Main and Water streets, Reilly was the keen-eyed proprietor, and Johnny Mack his genial manager. When they opened for the 1885 season in February they advertised an orchestra, nightly sparring matches, and a whole slew of performers who included Miss Louise Normand, the Petite Serio Comic, and Mr. Edward Kennedy, the Eccentric Irish Comedian, Vocalist and Dancer, in a Portfolio of Latest Songs.

It was likely around the same era, because he bowed out in Belfast in 1896 when he was 72, that the world's greatest tightrope walker, the fantastic Frenchman Blondin, appeared in Gloucester. His given name was Jean Francois Gravelet, and he startled the universe in 1859 by crossing Niagara Falls on an 1,100-foot tightrope 160 feet above the roaring water, later varying the feat by wearing a blindfold, doing it tied up in a sack, carrying a man on his back and what not.

But in Gloucester, as Brennan heard it, Blondin just coasted. He merely walked a slack wire strung a couple of stories up between two buildings across Main Street, trundling a wheelbarrow back and forth with a hot stove in it, cooking a steak.

"Ah, what a show town Gloucester was in the old days," reflects Jim. "One of the tops in the east. All the big names came here. There were 26,000 in town and a barroom for every thousand. Red Light district. Honky-tonks. Theatres. Swarming with fishermen from all along the coast. Sailors. And when the towns up the line voted no license, the influx would be on Gloucester. I can see us kids now, watching the crowd parading with the lanterns over to the depot to catch the last train home. Aw, it's all silly stuff today with the kids. In them days most of the hell-raisin' was amongst the adults."

There was the night the brother of John Wilkes Booth, the actor Edwin Booth, played City Hall (Jim's Uncle Bill Brennan was his page) and when the crowd jeered in the middle of a speech, he roared out: "I'm not my brother's keeper!"

And the great heavy-weight boxing champion John L. Sullivan, the Boston Strong Boy on the downhill grade playing Simon Legree in "Uncle Tom's Cabin" — "and he quit," says Jim, "for he couldn't take them sneerin' at him. And that reminds me that all them old shows when they came to town would have a parade beforehand to drum up the excitement, and my pal Charlie McPhee and me one time before "Uncle Tom" got to lead the bloodhounds up Main Street, which got us in free."

Another idol of the day was Denman Thompson, who made famous the homespun Yankee farmer Josh Whitcomb in "The Old Homestead." Thompson, if Brennan's memory serves, brought "Way Down East" and "Country Fair" to the Union Hill Theatre.

The Union Hill — before my time, but they say it was something. Frank W. Lothrop, the ship chandler, and James E. Tolman, provision dealer, who prior to that ran the theatre in the City Hall auditorium, opened "Gloucester's only opera house" just below where the new Gorton's office building is now on Main Street on the evening of

Friday, Sept. 7, 1900, with Hennessey LeRoyle in "Other People's Money." The Union Hill sat 975 and stood another 350, with a stage 50 feet wide and 37 feet deep, and 18,000 feet of rope and 250 blocks aloft to handle the scenery.

Some claim the Union Hill had the biggest stage north of Boston, and Frank Lothrop the biggest heart, with his reputation of being a soft touch on or off the circuit.

"Why that stage was so big," boasts Jim, "and Charlie McPhee will bear me out on this, because he lived just down the slope near Howard Blackburn's saloon and went to the Union Hill with our gang — it was so big that for the horse race in "Country Fair" they had real horses runnin' across it on a treadmill."

Down the street a few doors was the Dewey Theatre, a restless bistro that never stayed in one location very long and around the turn of the century met up with license problems; Mayor Merchant and one or two of the aldermen disapproved, at least publicly, of so much bare skin and bad talk all in one place in a town with such susceptible morals and tender sensibilities as Gloucester.

"The sophisticated bunch went to the Union Hill, and the more earthy crowd to the Dewey where they had all that stuff plus dancin' and amateur nights," says Brennan. "You know what I mean, like log sawing contests on stage where some wise guy slips a spike into the other guy's stick o' wood, and there he is gettin' redder and redder and sawin' away and goin' nowhere."

III

BILL KELLEHER, JIM'S OLD MAN'S vaudeville sidekick, went legit and opened a barroom. Long after the founder was gone, the show biz aura hung on. A few years back, Ed Flynn, a long-shot candidate for the city council, tried to ride a dark horse up the stairs for a drink on election eve. Neither his mount nor he made it, though he did get on when a vancancy opened up.

I guess everybody called him "Kellyer." Jim did, anyway. "You know, people would say down street, they'd say, 'Never mind the council, Kellyer's runnin' Gloucester.' I mean, politically he was in. They'd raid him when Prohibition was on, and

the customers would dump the stuff down the sink. So the cops would open the trap and drain off the evidence.

"Well, Kellyer got John Casey the plumber to rig the trap so it wouldn't hold anything. Next time the marshal showed up Casey had a glass in his hand and said 'You can't get what I got' and tossed it down. They went for the trap, but there weren't nothin' in it. Kellyer laughed like hell. I tell you, he was a connivin' politician."

Jim uses connivin' in eulogy. After William H. Kelleher, that imposing figure, died in 1937, Ira Marshall took the place over, pal "Iry" the one-time tumbler and wax museum curator. Another of his bartenders was Circus John Burns, to tell him apart from the other John Burns in Gloucester, Circus John having toured Europe with one of the big tent shows, perhaps Barnum and Bailey, as a buyer (of provisions, not elephants).

Speaking easy, as we were, of the Ignoble Experiment, Jim tells of the prominent Gloucester skipper who was in so good that when he offloaded in New York (and it was the best — straight Scotch from St. Pierre et

Miquelon — none of that hilly-billy stuff) the pier gate and his privacy were guarded by a squad of Gotham's Finest.

Uncle Bill Brennan was a runner and an oarsman and an early enthusiast for the Gloucester Athletic Club, whose gymnasium was above Shepherd's Market on Elm Street. Jim Connolly, the writer from Southie who quit Harvard to win the first gold medal (hop, step and jump) in the first modern Olympics in Athens in 1896, had his first sniff of the Gloucester he would love and immortalize soon thereafter. Dr. George Newell, Gloucester dentist and president of the GAC, enticed Connolly down, for a short time, to be its athletic director at 25 bucks a week — but mainly to organize, coach and play on the club's football team. This was around 1899.

Uncle Bill's oarsmanship had a part in inspiring Nathaniel Webster, owner of the Webster Block backing on the gym, to found and finance the Webster Boat Club which, if Jim remembers right, was over at the town landing. They bought a four-oared racing shell and put together a crack crew consisting of Uncle Bill, Dick Reilly, Jim

Mullins and another muscleman, and then they challenged the fastest four on the Charles River.

The city boys arrived in Gloucester with their shell, all ready to show the fishermen how to make chowder. They even brought along a victory bouquet — for themselves. The two shells raced in the harbor off Pavilion Beach, and the Gloucestermen won. The Boston guys were so mad they went home with their flowers.

This Nathaniel Webster's show business aspirations didn't come off so well. He was a smart businessman in fish and ice among other lines, though somewhat eccentric. He owned the Webster Hotel on Pleasant Street between the Customs House-Post Office at Fisherman's Corner (later Woolworth's) and the frame house and office of my grandfather, Dr. J. Everett Garland, known as the Captain's House. In the early 1890's Nat had this wooden structure moved up in town to Liberty Street. He remained inside the whole way, according to Brennan, and when he and his hostelry got there announced: "At last Webster has found Liberty. "

In its place he built in 1893

the three-story brick Webster Block, with an "opera house" on the top floor. It nigh touched Grandfather's place and rose high above it, which may be the cause of the "Garland/Webster feud" Jim heard about as a boy. Dr. Garland was known and a bit feared for his short fuse, as when the Salvation Army band was giving the Lord the fortissimo outside one day and he flung open his door and shouted to the lieutenant: "I'll give you ten dollars if you'll get that goddam band off this street! " The stunned Sally dropped to his knees and prayed for such a blasphemer . . . and he a man of healing too. Of course Grandpa was a Unitarian, which explains a lot.

But Unitarian or not, he wouldn't go so far as to torch off his neighbor's property at the risk of his own. It was the night of February 19, 1897, when the upper two stories of the Webster Block went up in a burst of fire and smoke. Thousands jammed the streets to watch. While the firemen got it under control — and a remarkable job, too — the Gloucester High School Cadets in double-quick time evacuated every piece of furniture and all the valuables

from Dr. Garland's (he was a school committeeman . . . besides having brought most of them, probably, into the world).

Old Webster, ailing and bedridden in his apartment in his block, was evacuated by force, for he swore he would mingle his ashes with those of his theatrical dreams and had to be carried bodily out of his smoke-filled chamber by firemen and friends. He died less than three years later at 70.

And then there was the time Jim Brennan senior was running an act at City Hall. "There was this sort of a character around town, Luke Brophy, a junk dealer. He mostly scrapped old fishing boats. Brophy was all right, but he had a lot of mouth — talk, talk, talk — and he kept pesterin' my Pa for a part.

"So finally he said OK, and they strung a wire from the balcony in the auditorium down onto the stage, and he told him at the cue 'when I say — I cannot expect Mr. Brophy tonight, but I think I'll get a wire from him — when I say WIRE, you slide!'

"Well, that night Brophy slid down the wire over the au-

Stuffy McInnis

dience's heads and landed in a heap on the stage and damn near broke his neck, but he was all right.

"Yup, the old man was a real conniver for show business."

IV

JIM WAS BORN IN A HOUSE AT THE rear of 47 Warner Street up in the center of Gloucester. Steve McInnis was a call fireman with the Colonel Allen Hook and Ladder Company, Number 1, and a teamster for Cunningham and Thompson, the fish firm, and had the house on the street and five boys. Mrs. McInnis took in fishermen boarders. They'd kid around with John, specially, who was eight or nine — "that's the stuff, Johnny," they'd say, "that's the stuff."

So Brennan tells it, and Stuffy McInnis grew up to be probably the greatest fielding first baseman of all time. So say his grizzled partisans, more fiercely loyal than ever, twelve years after his death.

What a record! In fifteen years at first base in the majors, 116 errors in 18,735 chances, and a lifetime batting average in 2,128 games of .308. Lesser men are in the Hall of Fame, the old-

sters argue. Why not John Phelan McInnis?

All the brothers were athletes. Jim the eldest, a good baseball and basketball player with the New England League; then Steve junior, and Stuffy, and redheaded Albert (Brick) and Bill, both ballplayers.

But Stuff was the star, all five foot eight inches of him. Jim remembers that he got started on Burnham Field in the next block, then on to Gloucester High where he took over shortstop, then to the Beverly town team, and then Haverhill in the New England League at a hundred bucks a month, where Cornelius McGillicuddy, himself a graduate of the League from behind the plate, caught up with him.

The kid was only 18 that season of 1908. Connie Mack took him south with Philadelphia for spring training in 1909. For two seasons he played at short for the Athletics, not brilliantly. But Mister Mack saw the genius in him. Harry Davis's time was running out at first. The manager retrained Stuff and put him in for the veteran in midstream of 1911. It was a slow start, but by 1913 McInnis was on the road to immortality if not to Cooperstown.

When the hometown boy joined the A's the city put on a testimonial for him, recalls a schoolmate, Al Flygare, the last of the Gloucester sail makers. It was to be up at the Union Hill Theatre. They'd been selling tickets for a couple of months, and there were speakers lined up, and the usual gifts. But when the big night came, no Stuffy.

They were desperate. "Mebbe he's gone to Manchester to see his girl," somebody thought, so they hightailed it up Western Avenue, and sure enough there was the pride of Gloucester trudging along past the Hammond place. "They grabbed him and rushed him back and shoved him out on the stage," says Flygare. "He was some sheepish. Cool as anything in the ball park with tens of thousands watching, but too bashful to get up there in front of the folks in his own town."

Webster's Field was abandoned sometime after 1920, when the trolley company quit, but ah, the ghosts that stalk that wild place of brush and meadow off the Nugent Stretch over the line in Rockport. The ball field was toward Cape Pond, bleach-ers behind the first and third base lines that would hold a couple of thousand, and some of the hottest semipro ball anywhere.

The old men reel off the names and savor them like a puff on a favorite pipe — the New England League, Stuffy McInnis, and Everett Perkins who played for Fall River, and his brother Cy, the other Gloucester great who caught for the Athletics, both from Centennial Avenue — and Cy and Ty Cobb, and some others from the majors who'd occasionally be rung in to play — and Duffy Blatchford, and a pitcher Jim Brennan remembers as a minister's son from Peabody, a corker, who was in the big time and then quit and returned to semipro ball and probably made more money in the bargain.

The fans swarmed off at Webster's from the "Dude Train" of the B & M Railroad which paused at the now defunct Bass Rocks summer stop near the little Babson Museum . . . and from the 'round-Cape trolleys, the open electrics from Gloucester, every car bursting with passengers hanging on the sides and clinging to the roofs.

Both Jim Brennan and Al Flygare went to those games and were there the day the first-base bleachers collapsed, as was Al Joyce of Gloucester as a player, the same Joyce who later in 1920 topped the League with a .463 average and has an elegant cup to prove it.

Flygare: "It must have been around the start of the First War or before that I remember the teams playing. It was the Knights of King Arthur against the Rockport White Sox. The stands sort of rocked forward, and then back, and then down they went. Nobody was hurt real bad, but there was one guy who got caught on an upright that was left standing as the works fell and it hooked him under the back of his coat, and there he hung. They had to shinny up and cut him down."

Webster's Field. All gone. No more take-me-out-to-the-ball game. No more running down the railroad tracks to sneak in with the crowd, no more trolleys detrolleyed in a shower of sparks, no more trampled dust, no more the crack of the bat and the roar from three thousand parched throats. The high jinx, the anticipation, the vast excitement, the easy informality of the old semipro circuit when corking good ball came to the boondocks . . . it's all the reverie of the old men.

"Oh boy! " crackles Al Joyce, now 76, still plumping for Stuff for the Hall of Fame, "what times we had in the days of my youth!" And he crouches and swings an imaginary bat.

McInnis moved from one triumph to another and walked off the field in 1927 to coach Harvard, covered with glory. He had dominated first base for Connie Mack until 1917. Then he was with the Red Sox for four years. In 1922 he played for Cleveland, then back to Boston for two seasons with the Braves, tapering off with the Pittsburgh Pirates until his final season, when he played in only one game and helped manage them to the pennant in 1927.

Stuffy's special claim to Cooperstown was staked out between May 31, 1921, and June 2, 1922. First with the Red Sox and then with the Indians he established twin records at first base never equaled — 1,625 consecutive chances and 163 games without a single error. His runner-up is Frank (Buck) McCormick, playing in the Na-

tional League for the Phillies (thanks, Doc Enos, for the team, right outa your head!), errorless in 1,337 chances and 138 games in 1946. Furthermore, during the whole of those two seasons McInnis bumbled but six out of a grand total of 3,106 chances.

Many are the stories of the quiet one — of the home run he hit his first season at first base in 1911, off a warming-up pitcher while the A's and Red Sox were changing sides in the eighth inning, and it counted under a brand new ruling — and five years later, during another game with the Sox, when he got one of only five hits off the young pitcher Babe Ruth and then congratulated him in the hotel lobby after the game for his pitching. The Babe, who had a lousy memory for faces, looked Stuffy in the eye and replied: "Yeah kid, it was a pretty good game. Glad you could get out to the ballpark and see it."

Of the five world series he played in during during 19 years with the majors, his last in 1925 was fittingly his most dramatic. McInnis was 35. The old legs and the old arm weren't quite what they used to be, and during the season he was in but 59

games for the Pirates. They won the National League pennant, but Walter Johnson of the Senators pitched them into a corner at the very start of the series, and they were down three to one when Bill McKechnie acted on one of his managerial hunches, benched George Grantham and sent in the wise old Gloucester boy at first base.

The veteran from Warner Street knew every Senator like his brother. He whispered in the pitcher's ear as each stepped to the plate, commanded his own old ground with consummate virtuosity, and with a magic that would never be forgotten by those who were there, electrified his young teammates, turned the tide of defeat and sparked the Pirates to three straight victories and the championship of the world.

The next week, back in Gloucester, the schooner *Columbia* was off Eastern Point tuning up for the Fishermen's Races, and up in town a grand testimonial banquet was put on for the returning hero of the 1925 World Series, John Phelan McInnis.

This time he showed up.

V

AND NOW, GLOUCESTER IN THE FINALE OF STEAM BEFORE WORLD WAR I. TAKE IT JIM BRENNAN:

IN THEM DAYS THE MAIN FUNCtion of the tugs was towing the schooners to the wharves after they come in the stream, to take out the fish. And also taking them around to the marine railways — Rocky Neck, Parkhurst's, and Burnham's. When a vessel come in from a trip, she'd generally most always have a signal to put up in the rigging for the tug to come out by the Breakwater and the towboats had a lookout up on top of the old Steamboat Wharf.

Once inside the harbor, the tug would always come up alongside for the tow in, never towing astern. Same way taking a vessel out, alongside, then off the Breakwater she'd put up her mains'l and away she'd go. Very seldom used the long haul, the long hawser, unless to Boston or back.

Also generally they'd bring in the salt barques from Sicily — Trapani — which would come to anchor in what we called the Deep Hole off of Rocky Neck, between Pew's and Wonson's wharves. First the steam lighters

would take out some of the salt, to lighten 'em because they was too deep, fully laden, to come into the wharf; then the tug'd bring 'em the rest of the way.

The lighters was mostly old Tom Reed's at East Gloucester. The *Abbott Coffin* I remember, and one old-timer, the *Joe Call,* and the *Phillip*. The *Phillip* and the *Abbott Coffin* pumped water and they used them for fireboats too. Wooden, right wide open, not much capacity but enough to lug the salt over to Pew's or Parsons's at East Gloucester. All steam. Not so much propulsion as the towboats. Long booms. Steam boilers and h'istin' engines on deck, everything on deck.

In my time, for towboats

Eveleth assists a mackerel seiner with an embarrassment of staysail off Harbor Cove.

there was the *Eveleth, Nellie* and *Priscilla*. And the *Mariner,* she came a little later, had an outboard exhaust. Us kids got a kick out of watching her around the harbor, puffin' out the steam; but the others had condensers, recirculated the water, and they didn't throw the steam like the *Mariner.*

Charlie Heberle, Cap Heberle, built the *Eveleth,* and Captain Andy Jacobs had her when I was a kid. My uncle was engineer on her, and the thing that always made me think how smart he was, his name was Crosby, and the gauge in the engine room said Crosby on it, and I thought he must be an awful smart man, he makes his own gauges. But it was made by the Chelsea Crosby Steam Gauge Company.

Cap Heberle had power steering on the *Eveleth*. A steam handle in the pilot house opened the valve that let in the steam piped from the main boiler to this little auxiliary engine which turned the wheel. For working in close quarters. The chains came down from the wheel and ran along deck to the rudder. When they were going hard over, you could hear them chains

rattlin' in the scuppers, turnin' the rudder. Had a bell system and speaking tube from the pilot house to the engine room. Bells and gongs. We kids used to get a kick out of listenin' to the gongs . . . signals for full speed, back up and all that.

The engine room was just about amidships. Next forrard was the boiler room, and forrard of that a kind of a mess or galley where the deckhand hung out. He was cook on the long hauls. Besides Captain Jacobs was my uncle, the engineer, fireman, and deckhand. Along with firin' the fireman had to come up on deck and help with the stern lines. Astern of the engine room was a slop place where they stowed cordage and stuff. The coal was kept both sides of the engine room, dumped into bunkers down through plates on deck. Pilot house was half round with windows on all sides so you could see out any part of it, with the big wheel in the middle.

Summers when school was out I'd take my uncle's lunch down to the boat to him, and sometimes he'd say, "Well, you can git a ride to Boston today." Going up, it would be a schooner with fish, lined up for a higher

price in Boston than Gloucester. Or maybe we'd go pick up a vessel had taken out at Boston and wanted to get home quick, because we could do twelve knots, and they couldn't hold to that the whole way under sail. I think the *Eveleth* only got about a hundred dollars for the tow, so it was worth it if there was enough price difference on the fish.

To bring 'em home, we'd pick 'em up at T-Wharf where they took out — most generally have to wait for some of the crew to come down from uptown. We'd pull away from the wharf amidships of the vessel, with lines fore and aft to her, and when we got out around by Deer Island, say Nixes Mate, we'd shift over to the long tow, with the hawser dippin' in the water astern. Captain Jacobs would holler through his megaphone, "H'ist yer fores'l!" to ease the strain of the tow, and they'd h'ist their fores'l.

There was some fun and excitement one time I remember, comin' down, they'd probably had a few drinks uptown, and after they h'isted their fores'l they decided to h'ist their mains'l too, and they did. Well, pretty soon the schooner was sailin' along, with the hawser splashin' through the water between us, right abreast of our pilot house, and Jacobs was hollerin' through his megaphone, and everybody excited, "Take in yer mains'l! Take in yer mains'l!"

Another good trip on the tug was to go through Squam River up to Essex to bring home a new vessel. After they knocked out the shores and the hull slid down the ways at high water — you'd have to catch the tides just right — we'd put a line on her and tow her astern out the Essex River and back around the long way, round the Cape. There was always a bunch on the vessel and a bunch on the tug, and it was a big day.

I was on the tug when the *Henry Ford* was la'nched in '22, when the hawser broke comin' out Essex River and she went on the beach. Had quite a job gettin' her off. The spars for the new schooners fitting out came to Gloucester from Oregon on the railroad and were dumped overboard at Thurston's spar yard up the head of Harbor Cove, for storage. You'd see a man with an adz there shaping 'em, and then they'd haul 'em over to the shears, about where

the Quincy Market wharf is now, the only place in the harbor where you could step masts.

One job everybody hated was working the barges with guano from South America or somewhere. Had to tow them into Vincent's Cove, which is all filled in since, to Dodd's plant to make fertilizer out of it. Awful stuff to have to get near to. Jim Black and me kept a Friendship sloop in the cove, at Sam Lane's fish wharf where the sword fishermen tied up. Charlie McPhee bought her from us and had her for years, and when they filled in they buried her in behind the North Shore Theatre where the parking lot is. That was quite a cove. There was Lane's there, and Friend's coal wharf, Bishop's ship yard, a shoe factory, the Olympia Theatre built on spiles at the west end of it, and numerous other things going on. The gang went swimmin' off Friend's. Used to be you could walk right off Main Street into Vincent's Cove. All gone now.

At the west entrance to the cove was the Boston Steamship Wharf. The *City of Gloucester*, mostly cargo, had the reputation of never missing a trip through all kinds of weather,

year round, and you could set your watch by her comin' in at four o'clock with a big freight from Boston. The street would be jammed with wagons, waiting. They unloaded and loaded over gangplanks, a couple of them, on her port side I think, fellers wheelin' it in and out on two-wheel, sometimes four-wheel, handcarts.

The *Cape Ann* was the excursion steamer, summers. Clean boat, very clean. Lots of staterooms. Place on the stern under a canopy for the orchestra. The trip down took maybe an hour and a half, and they advertised shore dinners and what not at Long Beach Pavilion. Made connections with the electric cars on Main Street at the foot of Chestnut.

In them days the Lehigh Valley Coal Company had their own ocean-going tugs. They'd arrive off Eastern Point with three or four coal barges in tow, some bound down east for Portland, some for Gloucester which they'd drop off at the Breakwater, and we'd go out in the towboat and pick 'em up and bring 'em into the coal wharf. After they were unloaded we'd tow 'em out again and they'd anchor on the Pancake Ground in the outer harbor and wait for the Lehigh tug to come by for 'em.

Most of 'em had families with the father, mother and kids living aboard, and one time out on the Pancake we see a kid wavin' at us on the barge, and his mother was hangin' out the wash. Next day they was picked up in tow and dropped off at Hyannis. This was the First War. Up come a German submarine, and the nutty German shelled Hyannis, and the kid on the barge stood up in the stern and waved the American flag at 'em. It made quite a story around here.

Then there was the steam ferry, the *Little Giant*. She run between Hayes Landing in town, the end of Rocky Neck, and East Gloucester Square. One day she was going by the Atlantic Halibut Wharf, and there was a southeaster making quite a ground swell inside the harbor. We said she'll never make it. But she did. They took the steam engine out of her later and put it in a gillnetter, I think it was Captain Albert Arnold's.

You couldn't wear out a steam engine. For haulin' vessels, Burnham's railways had a hor-

izontal slide valve steam engine that come out of a Mississippi River torpedo boat after the Civil War. Us kids all knew it.

Then after the steam, came the diesel. I did lots of work on the *Wanderer*. She was built around here by a rich hosiery maker, in the shape of a dragger because he wanted her to look like a workboat, but I called it a yacht. I piped up five engines in her before we found one that satisfied him. I piped up a Fairbanks Morse diesel one time, and we tried her out around Thacher's Island. Along came another vessel and was keeping up alongside, and then went ahead of us.

"Take this thing out," he says. "Put in another one. Put in an Atlas." We got back to Gloucester. He had a private train waiting for him. "I'll be back," he says. And he was. That man made a lot of work around here.

February 5 and 19, March 4 and 18, 1972; February 9, 1974

During the summer of 1973 Jim phoned me two or three times a week, gasping for breath, to damn "that Nixon an' all his gang," and to inquire after my Old Man, who

was also very ill and dyspneic. Regrettably I was too busy and preoccupied to get the "steam tape" into print so he could see it.

My father died on August 4. About five weeks later I called up to see how Jim was, and they were waiting for the ambulance. His daughter brought the phone to him. He gasped a few faint words into it, and died four days later on September 16. I was privileged to be a pallbearer.

29. He wanted a whiff o' Gloucester

LOUIE RICH WAS HIS NAME. HE was a long drink o' water, all freckles and a great grin and not the sign of a care in his 25 years. He rowed into the Independent Fisheries wharf out of nowhere and tied up.

It was a couple of weeks before the trials between the Gloucester schooners *Gertrude L. Thebaud* and *Elsie* to see which was going to sail down to Halifax and take the Fishermen's Cup away from the Lunenburg salt-banker *Bluenose*.

This was 1931, the end of September, and Louie was Rich all right — he was flat broke. The kid had picked up odd jobs in Gloucester a while earlier, and then he shifted down east to try his luck on a farm in Ellsworth. But around the middle of the summer he hankered for a whiff o' Gloucester again. He blew his last five bucks on an

old skiff and a new pair of shoes and shoved off.

A seagoing panhandler. The Depression was just sinking its teeth into things. Louie oared along up the shore, putting in to sleep on a beach here and a lawn there, under the stars, or at Coast Guard stations, bumming his meals or going without, sometimes just tying up to buoys.

Two hundred and fifty miles along the ins and outs of the Maine coast and a month of rowing, and then one day the Coasties picked him up, drifting and exhausted in Ipswich Bay, and took him to the Plum Island station. After a long kink of sleep and two or three squares, he rowed on through Squam River and into Gloucester.

Happy-go-lucky Louie, trading on his day of fame, talked himself aboard of the *Thebaud* while she beat the gallant *Elsie*

two straight, and he got the race fever along with all the rest of Gloucester. He was down there every day hanging around the Atlantic Supply wharf, badgering Captain Ben Pine. As he watched the stores going aboard for the trip to Halifax, hunger urged him on.

"Cripes, Cap'n Pine," said he, "I'd sure like to make that trip! I never saw so much corned beef and cabbage in my life. Gee, that's a fine bunch o' grub!"

The skipper of the *Thebaud* seemed to pay him no mind, went on bossing the work.

Louie edged closer. "Know what I mean?" he chuckled, digging his boney elbow into Piney's ribs. "Do ya? That's gonna be a swell trip, I'll tell ya." No response.

But when the black and beautiful schooner cleared the Breakwater and put her head

Captain Ben Pine at the helm of the Gertrude L. Thebaud, *1938*

to the eastward, there was the kid aboard of the pride of Gloucester after all. Captain Pine, ailing somewhat, had relented before he entrained for Halifax, giving the command to Captain John Matheson, who had been at the helm against *Elsie*.

Louie paid for his passage in laughs for all hands. They were hardly at sea before Nate MacLeod hung the nickname "Rownomore" on him and from that uproarious moment he was "Rownomore Rich", a regular mascot for the Americans, all full of jokes and cut-ups, puffing away at his harmonica, but sick as sin when it breezed up.

Rownomore bunked on the *Thebaud* , watched the races from the deck of the destroyer *USS Williamson*, and ate in the officers' mess with the newsmen and the bigwigs. When he wasn't too green around the gills, he scattered some gaity around the otherwise cheerless proceedings, for the big Novie fisherman left the American schooner in her wake twice in succession and kept the Cup.

The morning of the departure for home, Rownomore went ashore. Sailing time came and went, and they blasted the

foghorn for him until it ran out of air, but no sign. "Cast off," growled Captain Matheson. "We can't wait all day for him. He ought to be left if he don't know enough to be around."

It was a hard beat out of Halifax Harbor against a head wind and a lucky thing for the kid, too, for in an hour a motorboat overtook them, and there he was, standing amidships cool as you please, arms folded, looking like Washington crossing the Delaware. He sprang over the rail and disappeared below. Somebody on deck dug up his two dollars fare for the boatman.

Back in Gloucester reporter Roy Parsons wrote him up for the *Times*. But fame is fleeting. There was a bite to the wind and worse on the way. With no more work for Rownomore, he decided to head for Florida.

There happened to be lying at the Gas Company wharf the little old freighter *Ervin J. Luce*, about to depart with a load of Wingaersheek Beach sand for southern parts. Captain Bob Bailey took a liking to Louie and offered him and his skiff a lift as far as Bridgeport, Connecticut.

They crossed the Bay and put into Provincetown and then,

late in the afternoon of the eighth of November with a strong breeze out of the southwest, the *Luce* grounded on a shoal about 500 feet off Race Point. A patrol boat put out from the Wood End Coast Guard station, got a line aboard and dragged the sand carrier off.

But the heavily laden *Luce* had taken her death blow on that bar, and when they got her into the deep water, the tide and the wind took over and swung her into the rip. She wrenched, buckled and went down like a rock.

All four aboard, clad in their heavy clothing, leaped into the swirling seas. The Guardsmen sped up and threw out a line. One after another, Captain Bailey and his two crewmen were pulled aboard the rescuer.

Then they tossed the rope at the last, lone thrashing form of the passenger. It fell short. They hauled it in, and hurled it again, a desperate heave, snapping and arching over the waves toward the flailing figure. The end struck the water inches beyond the tips of his grasping fingers.

In one action, Rownomore Rich plucked at it, threw up his hands, and sank.

December 18, 1967

Running Free

30. Try splitting a March hare

BEFORE THE GREGORIAN CALENDAR was adopted, you will be fascinated to learn, this Martian month was the first month of the year, and in England up until 1752, today was legally New Year's Day.

This is a mad piece of news, to be sure, mad in the sense or nonsense of the March hare, meaning that hares go right ape during their breeding season, which is March.

Madness upon madness. I didn't know hares had a season on breeding. But my research tells me they do. Would you call an ill-bred rabbit an unruly hare?

March is the month of longeared lions and lambs, all right. The subject for some reason calls to mind the heroic voyage a year ago of Lewis Mills and his son in their 16-foot dory from the Head of the Harbor, out around the Breakwater and along off the Back Shore to a spot somewhat short of Milk Island, where after a Herculean struggle with the savage elements, they returned, battling the bitter biting winds and ice relentlessly, full of high courage, to their point of embarkation.

What an Odyssey!

Their plan, which they so unsuccessfully tried to keep secret from the prying newsmen, was to row across the Atlantic to Europe somewhere — they weren't particular — in 40 days.

They had studied the whole thing very carefully for days, if not weeks, and were outfitted for the ordeal. Blanket, compass, canvas, flares, two jackets, two pair cotton gloves, can opener, six inner tubes, and two pints of whiskey in case of capsize, prunes, stew, hash, cheese, crackers and a jar of peanut butter. And a saw. Mills threw in the saw as "we might have to cut the dory in half, my son take one half and I'd start rowing the other." And 35 half-gallons of water in glass jars. The mercury was 14. What'll you do if they freeze and break? "I guess we'll be in deep trouble."

"I'm glad they're finally going to go," Mrs. Mills told the *Boston Globe.* "I'm tired of hearing about it." What she told husband and son when they walked wearily back in the door that night is not recorded.

Getting back to what we were talking about, I have a thing about this mad miserable month, and so did Chaucer the poet, like maybe a speech defect:

When that Aprille with his shoures sote
The droghte of Marche hath perced to the rote.

Actually, Lewis Carroll had more of a thing about March than anybody. The Hatter did not

101

split hares when it came to covering them, and the rabbit was not one to welsh on an invitation out, so you will recall that when Alice came upon them, after being directed by the Cheshire Cat, the March Hare and the Hatter were taking tea at a table under a tree, using the Dormouse, who was fast asleep between them, as a sort of cushion.

What followed was the maddest tea party ever held, anywhere, any time, save for the one the Indians held on Boston Harbor, and they were mad as all get out, at the British.

Some dour, humorless, March type of reader, I suppose, is saying right now that this is a ridiculous column, an utter waste of time, but the same goes for this ridiculous month, a waste of 31 good days, with all its floods and blusters, scudding clouds and bouncing temperatures, and it must have been Julia Ward Howe who wrote:

The crimson flower
of battle blooms,
And solemn marches
fill the nights.

Well put, old girl . . . a very solemn month indeed, dark and foreboding, these March-filled nights, these night-filled Marches.

The mad month. The month of reassessments. The candidates have been reassessing, and the Assessors finally reassessed and admitted that the State Appellate Tax Board had been doing a little reassessing of the professional reassessors, Messrs. Cole, Layer and Trumble to the tune of $359,000 wiped off the books, thrown for a 14-grand tax loss.

And almost half as many again more appeals coming up next month. So will we have another agonizing reappraisal by a new set of re-reassessors reassessing the reassessors, all because Cold Layer of Trouble failed to take the trumble to qualify themselves to defend their reassessments before the State Board?

March madly marches on, and before us is spread the happy prospect of its successor, so cheerfully described by T.S. Eliot, that old Eastern Pointer, in "The Waste Land":

April is the cruelest month,
breeding
Lilacs out of dead land,
mixing
Memory and desire, stirring.

Dull roots with spring rain.

Which reminds me of the current word in the Nation's capital:

"It's going to get worse before it gets worse."

Or as they say here in Ward One, the Home of the Nuts:

"Cheer up — things couldn't be as bad as they are."

March 25, 1968

PS: Things got a lot better 19 years later in 1987 when I acquired a very sane little sloop charmingly named, quite coincidentally, March Hare.

31. WAVE, WING, SAIL — IT'S SPRING! ~~~

GLORY BE, IT'S SPRING! THEY'RE giving us a spring this year, at last, an honest-to-goodness spring, a hearable, smellable, seeable spring, one to put hope back in the old heart again, and spring in the faltering step.

How do I know this? Well, besides being a gorgeous weekend of soft sun and early popping buds, it was an ecumenical one combining Easter and Passover and the pagan rites of Demeter, and that's a triad of omens to be reckoned with.

Furthermore, it was a weekend pregnant with ornithological portent. I had the rare privilege of identifying within the space of 24 hours, a purple finch, a green-winged teal and John Kieran, famed Rockporter, writer, outdoorsman, and info-addict.

The purple finch was in the feeder swiping sunflower seeds from the chickadees, and I could tell what it was because it wasn't purple but the color of thin raspberry jam.

Teal and mate were dallying in the seaweed by the harbor rocks, pretty little duck types, and we could tell because Roger Tory Peterson's bird book said that's what they were. They were our first teals ever, migrating northward. Usually in such a case we call our neighbor, Sarah Robbins, the well-known naturalist at the Peabody Museum, in a burst of one-upsmanship to report our find and gloat, and she assures us she's had her eye on them for a week ... and they've been returning to this spot for nine years.

As for Mr. Kieran, the Sage of the Birdwatchers, there goes his stocky figure, trudging down the road toward the Eastern Point Light, benign, beretted and binoculared, in the company of some old crony, perhaps Dr. Mel Copeland, co-author of "The Saga of Cape Ann."

The finch, the teal and the Kieran, all three infallible signs that this year it will not be just one long March, but a genuine Cape Ann spring such as the home folks pine for, two weeks behind the mainland the way it's supposed to be, when all our fancies turn to love, or darn well ought to.

There were other symptoms of this wonderful epidemic called spring. The pheasant's squawk across the still, brown field ... a thumpeting flicker, winging away, showing the grey seat of his pants ... the unexpected flash, around a turn in the path, of fiery red swamp maple blossom ... old snapper turtle sundozing in the marsh ooze, bleary-eyed and cynical ...

A pair of pert robins on a worming expedition, peering sternly at Mother Earth . . . a scraggly flight of shags flapping north, honkless geese . . . slopes of shadbush on the verge of being triggered into bloom . . .

Fish crows bent on raucous errands to the edge of the tide . . . pairing gulls, making guileless, gullible love on the rocks, insuring future generations of gullkind . . . and a certain gentleness to the way the spring sea dies out on the sands.

And there was the vernal eclipse, a most relentless lunar mouthful on that starshot cloudless night — the fullest, coldest, craterest moon that you could reach up and grab out of the sky, so that it seemed a shame to erase such a bright light with such a bad black shadow.

But of course if you stayed up long enough, there it was again, peeping out from behind the silhouette cast by Europe, say. And just as the astronomers had predicted, our little heavenly companion was back as if nothing had happened.

And what surer sign than the first sail of spring? 'Twas a jolly Fishboat, skipping o'er the dancing harbor wave, pushed on toward nowhere by the sweet zephyr of the west, helmsman glancing aloft in that so characteristic mark of the sailorman's contentment.

So many signs of the cycle. The crack of the bat, the boyish shout, the quick flick of the dirty thumb sending the aggie on its way . . . the girlish squeal, the arcing jump rope . . .

The fresh-plowed field all black with receptivity . . . the first run of the fingerlings (and the gulls diving after them) . . . the throb of the lobsterboats consigning winter's cellar-made pots to the deep water.

Surf's up too. Wet-suited by the dozen, the guys hit Good Harbor Beach, from car to water in 30 seconds. The tide is right, the sun is warm, the girls are watching, and the tag end of a lazy easterly swell combs in around the jut of Bass Rocks.

They hand-paddle out on their boards, bellied or crouched, and when the big one surges in they hit the crest. Somehow the best of them suddenly are up in the white burst of froth, and surfing, exquisitely balanced, planing along on the smooth, advancing, whishing face of the wave.

They twist and turn and writhe, seem to lose it from under, but recover in a fast swing of the hips, arms akimbo. The really good ones ride the comber to where it curls around the bar, diminishes and dies, leaving them triumphant, standup victors on the wet sand.

Oh, to be 30 years younger!* What sport, what speed and grace, what thrills, what tests of endurance and strength, skill and courage! What fun!

Yes, this is the year of the spring. The world has paid for it with a long, hard winter of suffering and tragedy, and deserves it.

Hope springs eternal in the spring.

April 15, 1968

* Oh, to be 56 years younger!

32. QUI ME AMAT, AMET ET CANEM MEUM ⁓

THEY USED TO SAY BACK IN GOOD old Saint Bernard's time, *qui me amat, amet et canem meum* — dog latin for *love me, love my dog.*

Fair enough, and to even it up let's put a snatch of doggerel in the balance — "if I love you, my dog shall too."

Which about sums up the emotional pandemonium the leash-lovers have loosed, like the hounds of hell, on this most tolerant of communities. It is but the wind before the storm. The Council's public safety committee had better move its leash law hearing Wednesday to the high school auditorium — or up Dogtown.

The whole universe can be tumbling round our heads — war, famine and pestilence at our very doorsteps — and we placidly go about our small affairs. But let them threaten the status quo in the canine world, and we have at each other like

. . . well, a pack of dogs.

That's why we call him our best friend. "If you pick up a starving dog and make him prosperous," said Mark Twain glumly, "he will not bite you. This is the principal difference between a dog and a man." And he won't talk back, either.

Every dog is the mirror of its master's true self. Beware the man who beams at you while trying to restrain his alter ego from sinking its fangs into your shin. Give a break to the sourpuss with the friendly pooch. So it more or less follows that the way we treat our dogs as a minority group says a lot about the kind of place Gloucester is.

We have always been a pretty good dog town, ever since the old widows of the men who were lost at sea or in the Revolution had their pups up on the Commons for company and protection.

The dog population today is an independent lot. It has its yappers and yelpers, its howlers and growlers, a few snappers and fewer biters. Some chase after cars, some after girl dogs, and some just stand in the middle of the street watching the cars trying to get by. Some run to social gatherings, some are loners, some mind their own business, some mind mine. Some are purebreds, but most are products of the great melting pot.

About the same goes for the human population.

Round pegs and square holes. That's what I like about Gloucester, man and dog. As het up as I get when I'm in a hurry (and what's the use of rushing on Cape Ann?), I take a sort of contrary kick out of running the famous Bass Avenue Dog Pack that regulates the flow of traffic in and out of Ward I.

Often enough I've wished I had a dog, but experience has taught me that our ways of life are too different. I couldn't give another mutt the steady company he deserves, so I resist the temptation. And if we had to leash him where we live, in the open spaces, I would never get one. Next to Taunton, if memory serves, Gloucester has the greatest area of any city in Massachusetts, and probably the absolute lowest in population density — a lot of land for a dog to run on.

Who can doubt that an across-the-board leash law here would be honored more in the breach than in the observance, especially in the absence of a man with a net, and a pound?

The fewer restraints in a reasonably well ordered society, the better. May our City Council log a skillful and wise course through the puddles of poodly passion dead ahead that will preserve the rights of everyone, including the humans. Possibly there is enough law on the books already to protect these rights, including those of the dogs.

Police Chief Coyle, in his capacity as Dog Officer, ought to know more about our canine condition than anyone else in Gloucester, and his observations and recommendations in this essentially friendly fray should carry some authority. How enlightening it would be if the Chief might deign to deliver a State of the Dogdom Message before the City Council, and assembled factions of the citizenry!

Leash law hysteria is sweeping the Commonwealth, and many a community, I suspect, will soon enough regret having thrown in with this bitch hunt to deny all dogs their civil liberties for the transgressions of a few.

Sober reflection and the long view will surely prevail in old Gloucester. Our sensible lawmakers will conclude, probably, that the passage of new and repressive ordinances contributes less to the public good in the long run than the diligent enforcement of licensing and other existing measures that protect health and property from our more ill-trained or ill-natured friends.

We and our dogs have been able to get along pretty well in Gloucester for 350 years, and with some extra effort when needed we ought to be able to continue to.

The burden is on us, though. Are not the strongest bonds of friendship fashioned of neither thong nor chain?

May 20, 1968

The leash law passed after all, an animal control officer was appointed, Dogdom did not come tumbling down, and the Cape Ann Animal Aid Association seems to keep up with the slip-ups.

33. THE WORLD WAS THIRTY-FIVE FEET LONG ～ⱳⱳ～

WHAT A DAY SUNDAY WAS! WHAT a glorious day to wind up a glorious Fourth! What a day to take the old schooner out!

We raised sail around two and the wind was a shiver from the southeast, nothing to shout about, just enough air to take us around the Whistler and back.

So we swayed up the mainsail, and then the foresail and then the jumbo, dropped the mooring on the port tack, cleared the cove and let go the furling line on the jib, which took the wind with a fine flutter.

When we sheeted her in, *Bandit* nosed into the feathery water the way a frisky horse sort of chaws the bit. I hooked up the running backstay tackle and threw 185 pounds against the wire rope to the mastheads and cleated it down. Why, that jib stay twanged up half an octave!

Danced along, sweet and sedate, past the Breakwater and past the gas buoy, when right about abreast of Kettle Island, say, or maybe off Magnolia Point, instead of dying in its carpet slippers as we thought it would, the wind put on boots and freshened and kept freshening, holding steady out of the southeast, and there it was, a regular schooner breeze.

Perhaps it was a trifle more from the southard. Yes, I think it headed us somewhat as it came on fresh because we had to sheet in quite smart to shape a course between Baker's Island and Halfway Rock.

This was *Bandit* weather. She lay into it. Easy along on that port hitch, a real close reach, kept her lee rail dry, threw off a spatter of spray every now and then, but never a drop aboard except once when a teaspoonful ran down a sneaker.

Did she lay into it? I hope to tell you. The suds all white and asparkle in the glint of the westing sun frothed by, and they fizzed like sody water, and dipped down so gracefully under the caress of her counter, swooping back up from the hull lines to meet the wake of rudder-boiled bubbles.

And where the two waters met and merged they made a crest, a liquid calculus, as if you thawed out the solid geometry of a hard swirled snowdrift chiseled by a January northeaster.

Kept piping up, and before we knew it we were broad off Baker's, Halfway Rock up ahead to weather, but that was enough for one afternoon, so ready about and ahard alee.

She spanks up into the chop, dacron rattling. Let go the port running backstay and starboard jib sheet, bring her around

Schooner Bandit *gets under way in the Great Schooner Race, August 23, 1969, with Bill Sibley, Tom Morse and JEG.*

gentle, sway in your starboard runner and belt down the port sheet as the wind fills her on the other tack.

Easy, let her get her way on. No, it's a broad reach back to Gloucester, so we'll start all sheets and she can fall off as we do it. Now . . . that's it . . . full and by.

Look at her go. An honest seven knots. She's wild with it, plain joyful with the wind. A schooner wind if there ever was.

I mean she's boiling. Still dry as a bone, less heel now, driving home for Cape Ann on her best point of sailing, the best

for the whole schooner breed, the broad reach. Yes, it was the broad reach that put Gloucester on the map. You couldn't beat a Gloucesterman when the breeze was off his beam.

Bandit took us home as if every cop in creation was on her tail, and then we crisscrossed the harbor two or three times to let her sweat dry off before we made the mooring.

Yup, for three full hours the world was thirty-five feet long, and you could drive it, boy could you drive it!

July 8, 1968

34. THANKS, MR. CADY, FOR THOSE RABBITS ～ɯ～

THE PASSING OF THE VENERABLE and beloved Harrison Cady of Rockport this week sent me to my bookshelves looking for our mutual friend Peter Cottontail, but he seems to be missing.

I have a feeling that he took a little trip to the Morgan Memorial, when I think back on it, in which case Peter has some likely tot somewhere as wide-eyed over his pratfalls as he had me 40 years ago.

Getting on the track of rabbits reminded me that their literary proliferation began with a thin relic of innocence written long ago by Beatrix Potter called "The Tale of Peter Rabbit."

My heart still leaps into my larynx when I conjure up her scary picture of Mr. Mc-Gregor with his stickly whiskers all of a sudden plunging forth from abaft the cucumber flat, brandishing his rake at that tres-

passing rabbit in the radish patch. A raiser of radishes myself, my agricultural sympathies lean to McGregor. But not so in childish retrospect. Run, Peter, run!

Still, I like rabbits, I do, and not in stew, (out of the road, little cottontail!), and it was Thornton Burgess and Harrison Cady and Farmer Brown who picked up where Miss Potter and Mr. McGregor tired of the chase, bringing up the rear of my childhood.

If Mr. Cady is up there knocking, he and Saint Peter will get along just fine.

While beating the bushes of my shelves for Peter Rabbit, I discovered, not unexpectedly (knowing rabbits), that his cousins and uncles and various other relatives were lurking everywhere. As I suspected he might, who should pop out at me but a rather complacent

My old pal of about 65 years, in Pooh's Corner above my desk. New sweater knitted by Helen.

character whom I immediately recognized as the pal of another old friend, Mr. Winnie-the-Pooh. Now Pooh, the partisans of A.A. Milne will remember, was and is a chubbyish bruin known in the full formality of his dignity as Edward Bear, Esq., whose love of honey once got him into a famous and very tight squeeze. Pooh's and my consort of old who bounced out so officiously was named with that same presumption of posterity as befits the King of England and the Pope.

Rabbit. That was all. Rabbit. And the gang of my childhood was there with him — Christopher Robin, Piglet, Tigger, Eeyore (my parents sometimes called me Eeyore when I was a small boy, because I could always see the dark side of any cloud, even then), Kanga, Owl and the Heffalumps who never showed up.

This pleasant reunion at Pooh Corner brought to mind the time Christopher Robin went down to the market square with two bright pennies to buy a rabbit (rabbits again): "And I went to the stall where they sold fresh mackerel — ('Now then! Tuppence for a fresh-caught mackerel!') — 'Have you got a rabbit,

'cos I didn't like mackerel?' — But they hadn't got a rabbit, not anywhere there."

Well that was all right, 'cos I didn't like mackerel when I was very young either. But they let me have a white rabbit in the back yard, and it twitched its pinkly nose and nibbled fresh lettuce through the chicken wire.

But look here, who's this? Not another rabbit! Well as I live and breathe, so it is, and let me tell you, in a hurry too, hopping out, all business, from between "A Christmas Carol" and "Through the Looking Glass." You can see he has large affairs on his mind because he keeps pulling out his watch and peering at it, and he certainly is dressed for some formal occasion, perhaps a tea party, in a very tall beaver and morning coat. Indeed it's him, another old, and if I may say so, rapidly passing acquaintance, not the sort of rabbit you could really warm up to, a bit of an odd stick to tell the truth, known amongst the Warrens of Wonderland as The Mad Hatter.

Rabbits everywhere. Never saw the like of it. How can a writing person keep his library in order and know where every-

thing is when there's a rabbit peeking out twixt every other volume and . . . hold it!

What in de worl you doin' heah, Brer Rabbit? Thought I tole you ter stay in dat dere book til ole Remus let you out an nary a skimpitty minit sooner nohow an heah you be, ahoistin' up you ears, an agrinnin' at sumthin, an I know yer up ter no good. Git back in thar in dat book an stay!

An Brer Rabbit he git back in de book — til my back is turned. But Harrison Cady's Peter Cottontail and Reddy Fox and the rest of that flock of scamps he and Thornton Burgess and Beatrix Potter let loose are off the shelf and all over the landscape, and I reckon that's as close to immortality as any of us can git, don't you?

December 12, 1970

35. TO THAT MOST DELICATE AND SOPHISTICATED COVENANT ～m～

NOT MANY OF OUR PARENTS GET TO celebrate fifty years of marriage, and hardly any of us will if the divorce rate continues to rise faster than the life expectancy curve.

Golden wedding anniversaries are not common, and those happy enough to make the newspapers raise the inevitable question: how did they do it? A baffling proposition, considering that marriage is the most delicate and sophisticated covenant that two people on the face of this earth can embark on.

To round out the golden fifty, luck is an essential, the good luck to reach your seventies or eighties together. And wisdom, however that is reached, insight and good sense to realize that if no household can long stand divided against itself, neither can most men and women long suffer mutual servitude, voluntary or involuntary. These are necessary in-

gredients, but not sufficient. Add a pinch of chemistry, and you are off to a good start.

As for the rounding out, it is with renewed pleasure and the faintest glisten in my eye that I toast again my own father and mother on their first half a century of constant and intriguing rediscovery, joyfully reached September 20th. I thus raise my glass not with any deliberate intention of intruding on their privacy, but, if I may be pardoned, to vent a head of admiring filial steam, to shout it boyishly from the housetops: Hurray for you, Ma and Pa!

They met, I am informed by those earlier on the scene than I, while the young Gloucesterman, just graduated from Harvard Medical School, was in training at the Massachusetts General Hospital where the girl from New Hampshire was a nurse, head nurse of a ward in fact, at a mere

Ma and Pa and me, 1924

22, during the raging influenza epidemic of 1918.

It was a charming romance. They strolled and bicycled and motored in the Model T, watched the moon rise, shared their sandwiches with the ants and canoed on the Charles River, hiked and played croquet and so on, all really none of my business, and it all delighted their friends.

And what chivalry! At the most nervous height of the infamous Boston police strike in 1919, Pa put a pistol in his pocket when he took his girl out to dinner one dark and fearful night at the Wayside Inn in far off Sudbury.

They didn't rush things, and it was all of three years, I believe, before Joe and Mira pledged themselves to that covenant in the front parlor of the Crowell home in Concord, New Hampshire, fifty years ago.

In a year and ten days I made my appearance, and in six more years, my sister Anne. There were 25 years of the practice and teaching of pediatrics in the Boston area, through the twenties, the Depression and a war, and the whole family was involved, as a doctor's must be. Then another career for Dr. Garland the liter-

ary man — 20 more years as editor of *The New England Journal of Medicine.*

In all that time there have been good times and hard, travels, so many friends, accomplishment and recognition ... illness, limitations, deaths and disappointments. There has been growing old and taking stock, cutting back, shortening step but always moving on,

Pa and Ma, 1971

always zestful, always sharing.

A son so well-endowed parentally writes just short of the sentimental, he hopes. Time has rubbed away the rougher corners of a houseful of individualists. It is less difficult now to be less passionate.

She is so many good things to us, but through it all the nurse ... he, so many sided, unsure and sure, always the good physician. Both of them New England, coun-

try and coast, conscience driven and yet as humorous, looking in the mirrors of each other, as can be. And as amorous.

One is tempted to confound the role with the real thing, to attribute the success of the relationship to the mold in which it was poured, in their case a professional one. And it is true that they are doctor and nurse in some of the same ways that they are husband and wife and have been for fifty years.

On the face of it, that would seem to have been a neat and ready-made relationship that the young couple stepped into — almost a formula for a successful marriage — their common devotion to the needs of the sick and unfortunate.

That is part of it, but it is not the whole secret of this golden anniversary. The real secret, which is no secret at all, is that Pa and Ma brought to their lives together simply what they brought to their lives as individuals. So it would have been anyway, whatever their circumstances and the roles they chose, and so it is, even today.

And so, cheers! I say, and many happy returns!

October 9, 1971

36. WALKING IN THE WIND ALONG THE WINTRY BEACH —~~—

JUST BACK FROM A BRISK HIKE along Good Harbor Beach. By brisk I mean that it's a crackling winter day, the tide is out, the sun sulks in the south, the temperature is 21, and the wind is steady at 30 miles an hour from the northwest, which has quick-frozen my ears and the tip of my nose to about five below.

The snow lay packed underfoot above high water, and I had to lean inland toward the drifted dunes as I rather doggedly pushed along on a broad reach across the beach. Some of the low-lying sandstorms that whooshed over the flat to disappear in the dying surf, I find, found their way into my boots.

For once the sand was returning to the sea. I like the way the offshore blow flattens out an onshore swell and flicks off the crests of the breakers, waves moving in, and spindrift out . . .

an isometric match of the elements, wind pitted against water for a change, instead of ceaselessly urging it on.

Three herring gulls stared bleakly at me and resumed their aimless pecking amid the leavings of the tidal wash. Starvation diet, I thought. Why aren't these loners up in the harbor with the rest of the gang and the garbage? Oho, and what was I doing there?

I'd supposed I'd have the beach to myself. What other nut would be out on such an eye-watering morning? I wiped my nose, pulled my wool cap over my poor ears and buttoned my collar, and urged myself on, bound to make it to Brier Neck before turning the other cheek to the Montreal Express.

On the way back, as I took the bite of it on the starboard side, coming at me from the other end of the shining sand

was a figure, at first a mirage, a solitary Bedouin afloat on his Sahara, but as it shaped up and settled down, a jogger. He pounded steadily toward me, just skirting the rim of the tide. He approached and I prepared a cheery greeting. He was clad in pants and sweatshirt and sneakers, no hat, no gloves, eyes intent on the far edge of the beach by Salt Island.

He passed within six feet, unseeing, unsmiling, unfeeling on his Arctic jog, unspeaking . . . and the greeting froze on my lips.

Two strangers met in the middle of the winter in the middle of the place where sea meets earth, and exchanged not a word, not even a recognition of common species. Lonelier than three gulls. Like two planets we passed, each preoccupied with his own orbit. So be it, I mumbled frigidly to myself, though it shouldn't be. And it needn't.

A certain promising young lawyer in Gloucester jogs a few miles every morning around seven or some such beastly hour, all around the Back Shore and then along East Main Street to home, come high water, come low, sometimes dripping wet, sometimes crowned with a laurel thatch of snow.

But with a great joyous stride, and always with windmill arms waving to the right and fluttering to the left at friends passing in their cars, commencing their sleepy commute, always a cheerful shout, a flashing smile for every one. You might think he was running, or jogging, for public office. He keeps slim and trim. But he would be anyway.

A jogger of a different gait and weight, and older, stumps stolidly down the road to the lighthouse when the weather suits him, early in the morning before he leaves for Boston and his brokerage. If he spies activity in the kitchen he may wheel around the driveway and startle me over my bowl of Corn Flakes with a gasped "Hi Joe," as if he were delivering to

Athens, with his final breath, news from Marathon. He passes, and his dreary footsteps fade around the curve.

The serious jogger, except for the laughing lawyer, strikes me as a strangely masochistic type of flagellant who takes a pleasure I don't understand in the public mortification of his flesh and feet — a rather sad figure, a plugging, plodding, perspiring perseverer, scarcely able to put one foot before the other from fatigue as he belts himself along the highway. His arms wobble with weariness, his eyes are glazed, his belly flounces flaccidly. Sweat-streaked, oblivious, running whence and where he knows not, he lurches on against the flow of traffic and humanity in a semicoma of self-torture.

To what purpose is difficult to say. Your typical jogger, I assume, returns to his doorstep on his hands and knees and collapses within reach of a platter of scrambled eggs, a rasher of bacon, bowl of oatmeal, brace of sausages, toasted English and two cups of coffee, with.

Save for my windmill legal friend, none of these pitiful peripatetics runs for the love of

it. They detest every step of their self-ordained ordeal, and they're so bushed at the end that they doze half the day away at their desks.

Tears they may shed aplenty, but pounds rarely, since the inner man can never catch up with the outer. It is a useless form of exercise, painfully stripped of a single redeeming feature, not even a view of the passing scene, to which all joggers I've ever met up with are dazedly turned off.

Furthermore, this jogging must be positively dangerous, for once man has stepped onto the treadmill, how dare he step off? He must keep it up, day in and out, all weather and all year, keeping the tone in those leg muscles, the ones our primate ancestors employed when they first descended from the trees, building up capacious lungs and enlarged heart to accommodate the unaccustomed surge of circulation and rush of respiration that accompany his unseemly physiological trespasses on our pavements.

On and on he pants through his private nightmare of the dawn, because if he stops for whatever reason — if flu decks him or if his desperate wife hides his sneakers, or if in the utmost extremes of his delusion reason should intervene — if he knocks it off, what then?

Those magnificent, worthless, bulging gastrocnemius muscles of the calf grow soft, and that bouncing belly, no longer bouncing, merely bellies, and that great heart, relieved of its alien burden, retreats behind a wall of fat. And then where is your ex-jogger? Worse off than when he started.

Sorry, joggers, but instead of liberating yourselves from your flesh you have allowed, nay begged it to impose on you a brand of slavery so exquisitely horrible that, if you must know, the boulevards of hell, paved as they are with good intentions, have been worn smooth a thousand times over by sinners solicited there by yon corpulent Satan, and then sentenced to jog into eternity, in overshoes.

You're damned if you start, you see, and damned if you stop. Of course, as Grandpa Kenyon says, if you'd kept the woodbox filled from the forest you wouldn't of had to in the first place.

January 8, 1972

37. QUOTH THE WARBLER:

WITCHITY-WITCHITY-WHITCHITY-WITCH

IT ALL BEGAN INNOCENTLY enough seven years ago. I was having my usual difficulties writing a book and had the window open by my typewriter, not for jumping out of, but for letting fresh air in to clear the addled head, when one sweet morning I first heard this bird.

It was hidden in the emerging foliage in the garden, and the song was unfamiliar to me. Evidently a tiny thing, it didn't thrill "tit-willow, tit-willow, tit-willow," neither did it croak "nevermore," nor creak "kweek-kik-ik-ik-ik-ik," bald eagle style.

It sang and I quote: "Witchity-witchity-whitchity-witch." (Note the interpolation of the additional "h" in the third repeat of the main theme.)

Charming, I thought, if a trifle shrill, and returned to the problems of Chapter 11. And

there it went again: "witchity-witchity-whitchity-witch," a little closer this time. Insistent. It momentarily interrupted the frail thread of thought I was trying to follow on paper.

"Witchity-witchity-whitchity-witch," from another vantage. Insistent AND persistent. I got up and closed the window.

"Witchity-witchity-whitchity-witch." The muted flight of the offstage piccolo heralding the approach of the hero shepherd. However, I was not in a mood for Donizetti and tried to concentrate.

"Witchity-witchity-whitchity-witch." Jumped up, stormed downstairs, brewed a cup of black coffee, and back to the typewriter. Now let's see, where were we.

"Witchity-witchity-whitchity-witch." That did it.

The morning was dead. In less than an hour this newcomer to my scene had turned all my Franciscan goodwill into a smoldering irritation that would seethe and burgeon inside until . . . well, until . . .

Day after day, rain and shine, all the rest of that spring and into the summer, the creature taunted me as if sent by the devil. It never showed itself, remaining in one tree until I was on the point of absolute apoplexy. And then as I raised my eyes to the ceiling in appeal, temples throbbing, knuckles white, breath gagging in my throat, the song would cease. I would exhale deeply, fall back limp in my chair, all damp with sweat, and as I picked up the shattered pieces of my prose . . .

"Witchity-witchity-whitchity-witch."

The beastie had but taken

Yellow-throated warbler
(dendroica dominica)

advantage of my state of shock to flit soundless and invisible to its Station Number Eight. Witchity Station Eight for the bird. For me, at this rate, Section Eight and a jacket strait.

I timed it. Ah, how many times I clocked the regularity of that timeless song that never varied a note, not a nuance. The interval was nine seconds. Every nine seconds, from here, from there, from all around the place, commencing at dawn, ceasing — thank God for the grace of a night's sleep — at dusk.

"Witchity-witchity-whitchity-witch."

It was a hard summer, that summer of '65. I tried writing down cellar, and locked in the bathroom. I abandoned the typewriter and took pencil and paper to the secluded beach. I gathered up my notes and rowed out to the sailboat and threw myself on a bunk, slamming the companionway slide behind me. I ran screaming to the car and drove up the mountainside and tried to write, and into the fields, and buried myself in the library, laboring to put it all back together.

But I was a haunted man, and wherever I fled, within nine seconds of my return ... "Witchity-witchity-whitchity-witch."

Until one steaming August day something snapped inside. It was me or him. The hell with John James Audubon. Bird against book. My song against his. I lost control.

I dug out my old air rifle, filled my pockets with BB shot and went hunting. I stalked that song through honeysuckle and poison ivy, across the iris bed and into the catbrier, and at last I caught a glimpse of my tormentor, a scant flitting thing, clad in a suit of olive drab and dirty yellow. He fixed me with a beady baleful eye.

The old infantry soldier raised his gun and aimed with shaking hands ... hesitated, as well he might — then shut his eyes and squeezed the trigger. ZAP. A shattered leaf spiraled to the ground, and the target zipped off into a nearby maple tree, singing.

It was a day of infamy. For another hour that despicable figure of humanity dashed from shrub to shrub, taking cover behind fences and tree trunks, zapping to the right of him and zapping to the left of him, and the torn foliage fluttered silently to the earth, not at all like the gentle quality of mercy. His prey celebrated each new escape with the same old song.

"Witchity-witchity-whitchity-witch."

The last one was a clear shot into the bushes across the road. The little bird seemed to fly away strangely this time, with a hesitation, only a few feet before it disappeared from view. This time there was no song to signal another escape.

Had I actually hit it, winged it, or perhaps even inflicted a mortal wound? Had I silenced it forever? The hunter deep within me was overcome with remorse and shame. Was this harmless thing that knew but a single song lying deep in the brush, beating its wings, pumping out its life's blood?

Good lord, what had I done? I slunk back into the house and put away the air rifle, and could not work for the rest of the day.

And then next morning at breakfast, from across the road ... "Witchity."

Faint and feeble, but there it was. A solitary "witchity."

And I rejoiced. The day wore on, and another, and the whole song returned and gained strength, and I was happy in it. And as the summer waned, I ground my teeth sometimes, but stayed put and finished the book. Each succeeding spring for seven years, a bit less persistent with each passing season — for we have both learned to live and let live — my familiar friend has returned from wherever he goes in the fall to inform me, apparently, that he likes it here and bears no grudge. For my part, no more violence, and I have even librettoed another book to his predictable lyrics.

They're a couple, I think, and back again this spring. Never having succeeded in making more than a shooting acquaintance, I was astonished to run across him in full plumage the other day, eight feet away in a wild cherry tree. He had a white belly and a yellow breast and was wearing an incredible black mask across his face — unmistakably, I discovered upon consulting R.T. Peterson, the spring garb of the male yellow-throat, a warbler, with a song to match.

It was his mate I'd taken those pot shots at. Tsk, tsk.

"Witchity-witchity-whitchity-witch," he warbled cheerfully.

"Come again?" said I.

June 10, 1972

Bound Home

38. GOOD LUCK, TALBOT — YOU'LL NEED IT

FEW CITIES OF ITS SIZE HAVE BEEN *as fickle about self-government as Gloucester, swinging back and forth — according more to personality than to office — between strong mayor and no city manager, and city manager and titular mayor, all against an unpredictable rise and fall of charter changes. Nothing and nobody seems to make much difference.*

A man of few words, brusque Paul Talbot turned out to be the most competent of them all until he too ran out of political capital — but not out of town, where he still lives.

PAUL TALBOT
CITY MANAGER
GLOUCESTER, MASS.

DEAR MR. TALBOT:
WELCOME TO OUR UNFAIR CITY, from the drabness of our City Hall to the floating filth of our harbor, from our potholed streets to our rotten wharves, from our little army of unemployed to our dockbound little navy, from the depth of our apathy to the breadth of our cynicism.

Welcome to this fairest gem in the diadem of a sparkling coast, this rugged old bastion, this Home of the Cod, this once greatest fishing port under heaven, this still proud and dogged cape, this never-say-die, this Gloucester.

So much for the amenities.

From this day on, and so long as you hold down the corner office on Dale Avenue, you will be the most important, the most powerful single figure in this troubled, wonderful city of 26,000 very out-of-the-ordinary people.

We freely delegate to you this power.

Already you know a lot more about us than we do about you. Your credentials look good. You have the background, the youth, the training and the brains for the job, and you have been picked out of a large field by our new reform City Council.

You start with their confidence, and they still have ours. You have everything going for you. Plenty of people are saying that whatever you do will be for the better. You can make a national reputation in your profession by what you do here, and if you do it well enough we'll be happy to be your springboard.

You'll be well advised, Mr. Talbot — as I'm sure you have been — to play it very cool, as I'm sure you will, coming from more than three years in Old Town, Maine, where a person can freeze to death this time of the year if he opens his mouth too often.

Gloucester is a right peculiar place, a queer state of affairs to get the hang of. Political and economic factions, rival ethnic groups, the disparate interests of isolated communities, natives versus newcomers, natives versus summer folks, natives versus natives, and so on.

But you can get around all this with patience and good advice if you will recognize that the biggest thing you have going for you is that the vast majority of Gloucester people can agree on more than you might think, but chiefly on this: We are damn sick and tired of the way this city has been run for a long time, and we want some good government and we want it now.

We all know we have problems, big ones. And there isn't a man, woman, child or politician amongst us who has the answers, because this grand old place is reaping as it sowed, but more, is the victim of lousy circumstances and the whims of history.

The world has passed us by. But instead of crying "Stop the world, we want to get off," we're shouting "Stop the world, we want to get back on!"

That's where you come in. The only reason why your new

bosses got elected was because they told us they were going to try to give us a new deal in Gloucester. The key to that new deal was to be the hiring of an outside professional city manager.

Brother, you're it.

Mistakes we can live with; and before you're through, Mr. Manager, you're going to make your share.

Tough? Be as tough as you want to, but lay down the law where it needs to be laid. Do not treat the members of this City Council, regardless of your honest differences with them, as if they were any but the true representatives of the people to whom, through them, you are responsible.

Be as tough as you have to be with the leeches and slackers, the milkers at the public teat, the special pleaders, the back corridor artists, the machine pols and anyone who wants to make a deal because he knows somebody or is rich or landed.

But do not close your office door to the people or hold yourself unaccountable to the ones who are paying you to run their city. And do not play us for fools with fake tax rates, juggled budgets and the sly ap-

pointment of nitwits, nonentities and lackeys to bottleneck positions in your administration.

As I said, the biggest thing going for you is that the people of goodwill in Gloucester — which is practically everybody — wish you the best of luck and want you to succeed.

Public opinion is behind the new City Council, and it is behind you. It is a cynical and skeptical and much abused public opinion, but I sense that it is more aroused and more united than it has been since the advent of Plan E reform. That charter has been strained to the limit in recent years, and it is squarely up to you and the Council we have elected to prove that it can, after all, work as it is supposed to.

Our futures — and yours — depend on it. Good fishing.

March 11, 1968

39. THAT FEELING OF BEING CREPT UP ON

SEATED THERE IN THE COCKPIT OF this beautiful, modern, 1930 Triangle class sloop I've just dickered myself into, catching up on a small rigging chore, I thought . . . can anything in the world compare with an October morning on Cape Ann?

Oh, what a day! It was low water, and so clear for a change that when I rowed out to the mooring I could see sand dollars on the bottom. Hazy, warm, windless, the autumn colors firing out of the green that fringed the cove.

Then with a beastly, shattering, screaming roar, a jet fighter threw itself across the sky overhead and was gone out to sea in a wisp of kerosene smoke, leaving the harbor cringing under the noise.

Through the wake of this glorious achievement of man, one of God's modest produc-tions, a monarch butterfly, all black and orange, fluttered above the still water in regal aimless-ness — so it seemed — pushed or pulled by the wondrous instinct that moves its mod-cloaked race to seek the climes of South America this wondrous season of the year.

I mused on what happy and healthful effects it would feel from its passage through the airborne sulfurs of the Mass-achusetts Electric plant at Salem. And it occurred to me that this mild autumnal haze might not all be nature-made.

The mood soured some-what, and with a return of the irritation they provoke, I was aware of the insistent bleating of the electronic foghorns the Coast Guard has inflicted on Eastern Point and Ten Pound Island. What was the matter with our good old bells? What in hell right did some officious, rump-sprung, tone-deaf chaircrat in Washington think he had to pull them out by the roots in ex-change for this hooting cacoph-ony? Bah!

Glancing over the side, I saw no more sand dollars, though the tide was still on the ebb. A gooey glop of refuse-strewn gunk had drifted along and was spreading over the cove, perhaps from the city sewer bubbler, where gourmet fish-ermen like to angle for excre-ment-fed pollock and mack-erel, or from the inner harbor, which Gloucester officials pro-nounced so remarkably pure a week or so ago.

A couple of gulls, mewing, swept by. A diving shag popped to the surface, sending an un-dulation of ripples through the blanket of filth, and snapped his beak around in nervous, shag-gian surprise at his new surroundings.

The knuckleheaded rattle of a woodpecker echoed across the cove, the sun shone down warmly through whatever it was shining through, and as there still was no breeze, I was not for the moment to leeward of some man-made stench or other.

So I concluded not to count my blessings. It was still a more or less valid proposition that nothing, no nothing in the world, can compare with Cape Ann on a lazy October morning.

But we are on the edge of it. My God, aren't we on the edge.

Get up on high ground and gaze across the bay toward Boston, and where the city used to be, most any sunny day, the odds are that a yellow pall hangs off to the southeast as far as the eye can see. The poison is advancing on us, over the Mystic Bridge, up Route 1, almost to 128 now, from the tail ends of a million cars.

And by sea, on a southwest wind and inversion, blending with the emissions of the industrial North Shore, the stuff that Big Boston spews up is bearing down, joining chemical forces with the homegrown

niceties of our own fish plants and the exhausts of the slab boats and our draggers and workboats and so-called pleasure craft.

And try to imagine, if you have the stomach, what one mansize oil spill would do to Cape Ann — our ledges, our beaches, our salt rivers, our marshes, our fish, our flats, our wildlife, our boats, our waterfront — just one good whopper, one of those coastwise tankers that takes refuge in the harbor holing itself on Round Rock Shoal on an incoming tide.

Well, I reflected, wrapping up my chore aboard, there's truth to the old saw about the enemy you know . . . the stink you know may be rosier than the one you don't.

Worth a column maybe, a powerful piece about pollution, full of poignant contrasts between beauty and disaster, that feeling of being crept up on by slow, irreversible disaster.

Yes, by golly I'll do it.

I picked up around the boat, tossed the frayed rope ends, old tape, grease rag, used-up beer can and empty paper bag overboard, pumped out the bilge, left everything shipshape and oared back to shore. The lead

paragraph was already taking shape in my head.

"Seated there in the cockpit. . . ."

October 10, 1970

40. In Gloucester we back into the future ~~~

YOU COULD ROAST A SUCKLING pig on the parking lot of the Northshore Shopping Center as I write, but out here in the Atlantic toward the tip of Eastern Point the August sun that bakes the mainland is made bearable by the westerly, fresh from the air conditioner of Gloucester Harbor.

Mine is not a bad vantage place, where the good unyielding earth of Cape Ann meets the red-brown ledge above high water. The new rises of Boston shimmer vaguely through the haze on a range with the red light at the far end of Dog Bar Breakwater to the west. Nor'ard the old fish city spills complacently down to its tumbling waterfront, strangely unchanged in the few generations since it was the salt cod and mackerel capital of the universe.

Almost directly across the harbor is the strip of beach where those English darers of the Western Ocean landed the first of the codfish 348 years ago that sparked and then fueled the ravishment of God's country.

Roughly between my perch on the Point and that first settlement of the Bay Colony at the Stage, an airborne colony of gulls circles, flutters and dips down daintily on a yellow froth of harbor, gorging on what we refer to locally as The Shore Dinner.

This cornucopia is The Bubbler, the outlet of the pipeline from which surges to the surface the raw sewage of a city of 27,000 good and clean Americans and all their various works. The Bubbler offers charms beyond description for hungry fish, chiefly mackerel and pollock, as well as gulls, and for leisurely anglers who are not particular about the daily diet of their day's catch.

Well, deduct The Bubbler and throw in the heavens and the deep, the winged throng, the keen-prowed cleavers of the wave, the queer fogs, the January vapors, the rosy-fingered dawns, the theatrical sunsets, the twinkle twinkle of the lights at night, the groaner on the easterly, the twilight crickets, the gales, the spray, the bitter northwest blast . . . and all in all we have a fine observation post from which to survey friend and foe, the near and the far and the middle ground, and if one is so inclined, the intermingling of past, present and, presumably, future.

The presumption of times ahead, like our air-conditioned westerly, makes the heat of the present more acceptable, and the past more believable — marred as the outlook may be, again like the westerly breeze, by the prospect of having first to traverse the intervening bubblers of the world.

So look onward I say, and if you can through the emissions, upward. Face forward unflinching, and take for your example the same stern optimism that all his later years was the mark of one old fisherman, the longest face on the Gloucester waterfront of his time:

"Every day is one more nearer the end," sighed he. "At least they can't take *that* away from me!"

Hell, we don't face the future here; we back into it, like the skipper of a small dragger I know who on a wintry day sets his course, turns his rear to the wind and steers by his wake.

Gloucester is the perfect sideline, if not penalty box. It has character, singular and plural. It is contrary, as different as the two old Down East sisters, one as different as t'other, maddening, lovable, apathetic (never pathetic), cussed, durable, weatherful, wonderful, flavorful and so distinctive that you can smell it, oh verily you can.

Expatriates by force of negative economic pressure will vow to you that it's a good place to be from, preferable to being at. Yet they do come back after they've made good on the outside, not to die, but to be reborn.

Gloucester is all right to write from, too. And about, which for nearly four years off and on has been the main preoccupation of my former column in the *Gloucester Daily Times.*

I reckon that the same stream of consciousness will meander out of this typewriter through four newspapers as wandered through the one before, and the best part of it is that you can dip in or not as you please without missing much of the story. Like a continuous movie; hang in there long enough and the lines will sound familiar.

I'm afraid the older I grow the harder it gets to put together and then hold onto a consistent point of view about anything that matters, or seems to. But we don't give up as each day brings us nearer the end, though these be times to make the compass needle twirl.

Gloucester, at least, has always been one hell of a point of departure.

August 21, 1971

This piece inaugurated a weekly column in North Shore '71, *the weekend supplement of Essex County Newspapers edited by* Gloucester Times *old hand Paul Kenyon. Twenty-three years later I've discovered it's the chart, not the compass, that twirls.*

41. WHO HEEDS THE POET'S PLEAS? ~⎍~

IN GENERAL I'VE GOTTEN TO KNOW those I wanted to along the way, but one of my major regrets is our (well, the world's) poet Charles Olson, who died 24 years ago at 59. Arguably the most intriguing Cape Ann intellect of his time, early in our acquaintance this giant son of a summering Worcester postman invited me to "pic-nic!" with him in a local cemetery by the grave of a notable fishing figure of another era for whom we shared an admiration. How I wish I had! How crazy he was about Gloucester, and with what frequently abstruse fervor did he versify against our casual self-destructiveness!

My sardonic reaction to the poet's stifled pleas drew no response from him, but his hurt was conveyed. Had I taken him up on the pic-nic! I would probably not have written that column and surely wouldn't have had to wait a year after he was gone to express something of what I might have while he was alive.

OLSON IS AT IT AGAIN . . . THE prophet without honor, the Jeremiah of the Fort, the Quixote of Gloucester, tilting at the windmills of our guilt, telling us what we hear but won't listen to, after saving us from ourselves/each other . . . : "it's yours to lose beloved City."

I read you Charles, I do . . . "has Gloucester any enough of such like-minded persons to so effect its own self?" Yes, yes, we do, behind the woodwork, they're hiding in the plaster of the Mansfield house.

You threaten us, you pull a Peter Smith . . . "I dream and go if no such number do exist" (oh no you don't Olson, you'll never shake loose of this place, nor we of you.)

Yes, I read you. This is the meat of it . . . "lose love if you who live here have not eyes to wish for that which gone cannot be

brought back ever then again. You shall not even miss what you have lost" . . .

Poet, leave us alone, will you?

"You'll only yourself be bereft in ignorance of what you haven't even known."

Olson, why don't you give up? You're 0 for 3, about to make it 5. They knocked down Solomon's Temple, the Hardy-Parsons wing and the Parsons-Morse house, and you couldn't stop 'em. Tally wants to fill the Essex Avenue marsh, and where are your troops? He wants to hot-top the Mansfield house, and where is your human barricade?

And you were wrong, Charles. Solomon's Temple had to go because the Y is doing more for our beloved City. The Hardy-Parsons shack was an ugly afterthought, and now the house is virginal again, and gardened, and the Parsons-Morse place — broken-down, really, no proud relic at all — and one of the few creditable things the last Council did was to hold off destruction out of deference to you, oh Poet.

Tally's marsh. Only the state can halt the fill, or $16,000, like for the Window. Only if productive can they save it . . . useful . . . functional . . . finger-lickin good. Beauty, the land and sea, the way Gloucester people live . . . what do they mean if you can't raise the dough?

Where is it all going to come from, oh Poet? I know how the kids used to sift through the barroom sawdust thrown out back of Drunken Street after the day's stray change. Do we shake our ashes for it? Will it come out of the hold, as they say?

Where is the dough to raise Phoenix or even hell on Rogers Street, to restore Ten Pound Island and the Fitz Lane House, to fix the Depot, to save Thomas Sail Loft (last around anywhere) to keep the sch. *Caviare** from sailing out of town (to like Des Moines where they love us), to do right by Howard Blackburn's old bar (oh the most

famous drinking place between Boston and Halifax in its time, now occupied by the Green Tavern.

Where, Poet, where? Where do we dig it up to build the new schools, to give the kids a gym and stadium and skating rink and get rid of the tin soldier ROTC, to build the new library and put books in it, and the new police station and courthouse, to get the water you can drink and enough of it, the sewage treatment and city pier, a list as long as your arm?

I'll tell you where we get it from, oh Maximus . . . from out of the hold, where we have for 345 years, and there's just so much of it to go round.

And that's the Gloucester story. Maybe things will change one day, and the big city will bring in the rapid transit and the big spenders, and the urban monster will advance with open mouth and there will be a big fat nutritious infusion of money and nothing else.

But not today, thank God, and not tomorrow either. Today there are fewer Gloucester people than 80 years ago, and taken all in all, this is a poor

place, as any place is that lives off the bounty of the sea and Unemployment . . . and it still comes out of the hold, whether it's yellowtail, lobster, greysole, market cod or scrod or a trillion pounds of frozen blocks.

You say . . . "without breath the young without even knowing why go anywhere to leave what itself has no attraction. It is doom this city is asking for, debris and doom, easily."

And I say how right you are, Olson, and how wrong. It is debris and doom Gloucester flirts with, yes, always . . . and elsewhere for the young to go if not to sea or close by, and come back to.

So leave us give them something more, the young, than the Mansfield house or even my thing, Blackburn's bar.

Let us pour out to them the guts of Gloucester, and to hell with the shells of it.

January 29, 1968

* *Mistakenly identified at first. Actually the* Lettie G. Howard.

42. A POSTHUMOUS PIC-NIC! WITH OLSON ⚯

CHARLES OLSON, THAT GREAT RUM-bling, rambling presence that made waves from Fort Square to wherever poets gather in the world, died of cancer a year ago tomorrow.

He was only 59, and on his deathbed he told his friend and fellow poet Vincent Ferrini that he wished he could have had 10 more years to look and listen and write.

But Charles had neglected or squandered himself after Betty, his second wife, was killed in a car crash in 1964. More and more he drank too much, smoked too much, and by turns starved and stuffed his massive body until finally it capitulated to the excesses of the genius lodged within it.

I hardly knew him, really, because I am ill at ease with people so big and overshadowing, and he was 6-foot-8, with brain and heart to match.

Strangely, or perhaps not, though we lived within sight across Gloucester Harbor, our closest communication was by way of an occasional corre-spondence from which I was by far the gainer.

Olson wrote the most ex-traordinary letters in a hand that lurched, like his verse, all over whatever scrap of paper lay near-est his pen or pencil when the mood struck — cheap yellow sheets, pages torn from a note-book, envelopes, a ripped royalty statement, even the emptyings from the wastebasket, if he had one.

The free flow from that labyrinthine mind was wild and wonderful. After my second Gloucester book came out in the spring of 1966, Charles dashed off a charming, generous note in the course of which he remarked on our common admiration of the late Captain Joseph W. Collins, the fisheries expert of the last century:

"Also delighted to see you have Joseph Collins under your light. I go regularly as a matter of fact to his grave — Maybe you'd like to do that with me some day as a pic-nic! together. The last time, say a month ago, my companion was, I discov-ered, as once previously in Nova Scotia (about Shelburne maybe — or above, on the East Road to say Lunenburg), and a marvelous other time, when only he & I confronted each other, on a road in, in Yucatan to what's called jungle but is really woods — or, in this instance, as in fact where Collins is buried, a Sacred wood — only this fox a month ago saw me first! And what a flash he was gone in!"

Olson was Joycean, and

Charles Olson

Gloucester was his Dublin. His garret was his flat at 28 Fort Square. "The nature of my involvement in the subject Gloucester," he wrote me once, "keeps me always in Ward 4 and in Heaven simultaneously." He disliked having to go afield to lecture or teach.

I shan't get off on his innovative "projective" verse; some of it certainly turned me on (the Gloucester pieces, mostly), though more of it was so crammed with his helter-skelter obscurities that I couldn't tell the head from the tail.

He is a poet for the young, an abstractionist; you have to have flexibility of eye, mind, emotion, to dig his convolutions. Part of him never grew up. But Maximus, as he projected himself, is a great figure in the literature of Gloucester too, and will be recognized for that side of him eventually, even here.

What preoccupies me particularly on the first anniversary of his damnably premature death is Olson the man and Gloucester. Do you remember what a towering tantrum it put him into whenever they destroyed another of his dear old buildings, the tottering relics of his town, his laboratory?

Charles put it to me thus in response to my outrage at the city's highhanded burning of the lighthouse keeper's cottage on Ten Pound Island, where Winslow Homer painted 50 of his watercolors:

"The moment you make any step of the least sort toward tourism they've got you, and you're done for. Tokenism is what tourism, in our block, amounts to. You must fight for your own people and for simply the Gloucesterite's right to stare or putter about or have what he's used to: if you become historical, in the sense there's anything in our past except which is right now live goods, no matter, say, if, say, time too has deteriorated it, one does have a ground."

And he added as a snorting postscript: "One has to be strong as a goat & ultimately probably smell as bad to live at all, it seems, in the immediate progress of this Country."

Our poet could care less about preserving the dry leaves of the past, dusting off the skeletons, making museums. He yelled to keep the "right now live goods." I trust he would not have spurned Howard Blackburn's sloop *Great Republic*.

Graveyards for Charles were for pic-nics! amongst spirits that had something to whisper to the now.

He strove sporadically with his poet's weapons to keep the city from tearing down the old Parsons-Morse house on Western Avenue to widen a curve that was never widened after all, hoping to buy it in his impractical way, and of course he failed.

And he screamed to the *Times* when the Y pulled down "Solomon's Temple" on Middle Street, and he tried to stop the razing of the vintage Mansfield house with its twelve fireplaces in the West End. Since his death, the Thomas Sail Loft, where presided the other late Charlie Olsen, poet of the wind's wings, has gone too.

Each time, with the exception of the Fitz Hugh Lane House, the bulldozer has proved mightier than the pen.

Can such as the Blackburn Building and the West End be saved and restored as "live goods" — the once handsome Pilgrim House to the west and

north, and the continuous blocks of brick fronts dating back to 1831 after the first great fire, the grand old granite bank — that stretch from St. Peter's Club to the little Isabel Babson Library for expectant ladies?*

A year has passed since Charles Olson passed from among us, but I see him now in my mind's eye, stalking the streets in his odd raiment of capes and shawls and sweaters, throwing his huge arm over my shoulder, all rambling talk and rumbling laughter.

Olson was too big for us. Gloucester was too big for him. His last verse in his last major work before his death, "Maximum Poems IV, V, VI," was this:

I set out now
in a box upon the sea
                    January 9, 1971

*Fortunately, yes.

43. SPINDRIFT SPUN OFF IN A DECEMBER GALE ~~~

THURSDAY, 2 P.M. — HIGH WATER, and with it some of the more powerful surf we've had pounding along the Back Shore in recent years. The predicted gale is bearing down on us, the muscle of it somewhere offshore but giving Cape Ann a good shouldering. Not often have I seen such a buildup of seas in so few hours.

From my window the Breakwater is a long and illusory sea serpent, undulating hypnotically to the processional inundations of the swells. These gale-built waves are borne in on the high tide so loftily and so intent on their own destruction that they simply bury the obtrusive wall of granite in their passage with scarcely a splash of protest.

My lookout is around 40 feet above sea level, and I judge the crest of the swells off there outside the Breakwater-to-be about in line of sight with where the horizon should be if I could see it behind the spume. These are the swooping, peaking, greedy seas that made a stormy entry into Gloucester Harbor a hard chance in the days of the double reef, and especially before the Breakwater was finished in the years fore and aft of 1900. That churn of Atlantic beyond the lighthouse has been the irritated reaction, since the Ice Age at least, of the suddenly bottomed ocean swells, heaving up over Eastern Point Ledge inside the Number 4 nun buoy.

Further out, the Whistler shrieks in plaintive distress as much as warning.

Before the Breakwater was built on it, Dog Bar was the next shoal in from the ledge to frustrate the shoreward rush of green water . . . and then Round Rock Shoal in mid-channel between the bobbing sentinels of Can Seven and the Gas Buoy. The Army Engineers at first wanted to run the Breakwater right on out over Round Rock. But they were dissuaded by "local knowledge," and the seas crashing across it today continue a strangely fearsome spectacle.

A wave crest of 30 feet assumes a trough as deep, and I suppose the halfway mark is your true sounding. Roughly then, the trough of a 30-footer highballing over the shoalest part of Round Rock, which is 13 feet at mean low water and 22 1/2 with today's high tide, scoops up 15 feet of ocean, leaving a depth of but 7 1/2 in transit. The same sea would bare the shoal at low water.

A mere fathom more or less turns Round Rock into something to wonder at in these winter gales, and that's what the whole of the entrance to Gloucester

Schooner Lizzie Griffin, *blown aground on Black Bess Point, Gloucester Harbor, February 1, 1898.*

looked like when my Pa was a boy, from Point Ledge all across Dog Bar (where depths ranged to as shoal as four feet) and Round Rock — one continuous, crashing, roiling broth of breakers that shot spray into the air 50 and 75 feet.

Those seas barrelling round the Point have to shorten their span as they shallow. They arch their backs, scrape their bellies and blow their tops. And when the gale backs around to the norard and norwest, it snaps the spume from their snowy crests and spins it away in a vaporous cloud.

An awesome sight. More awesome yet aboard the dragger that just hove in from outside, lurching and plunging. Playtime to the gulls and terns, shags and ducks — and mealtime on goodies served up in the boiling surf.

Even behind its Breakwater the harbor jounces in these easterlies. The swells explode and rebound from the western ledges, surge back to the Point, slopping to and fro, dividing into a thousand small swells and surfs from Lighthouse Cove to Halfmoon Beach and way deep inside, where the vessels rise and fall and groan and crunch against the wharves.

Slurpy now, but imagine what it was before that protective barricade of granite was set across the shoals to break the seas. The undertow was something fierce, as many the vessel that took cover here with a falling glass found out. The outer harbor was all hazard on days like this. The surge would lift up a schooner anchored on the Pancake Ground from astern (for she would be head to the easterly), carry her ahead, slack on her cable. And then that undertow would recede and suck her back on her chain with a horrible wrench, enough to send a man sprawling I imagine, if he hadn't one hand for himself.

Many's the stranger to Gloucester in times of storm, thinking himself safe in the lee of Eastern Point, in this way saw his cable snapped or his anchor broken out by the backlash of the sea. Many's the vessel was thus carried helpless and barepoled by the gale ashore or onto the Dog Bar rocks or out to sea.

Only deep in the inner harbor of Gloucester could the prudent seafarer find safe anchorage, and even here, in the worst of storms, the most cautious skipper could end up with a pile of fractured frames and planking on someone's rocks.

Perhaps, in this season of blessings, we should define before we count, and then be thankful.

December 19, 1970

44. A TIME FOR CHILDREN TO REMIND THE GROWNUPS ~~~

MISS MARION SIBLEY
EAST GLOUCESTER

DEAR MARION:

Having known you for most of your eleven years, I am not at all surprised to find you defending Santa Claus, as you did in your very good letter to the editor in Wednesday's *Times*.

After all, your big brother and your two older sisters have been raised to speak their minds, and your younger sister Kate won't grow up to be a shrinking violet either, in my opinion.

Old Nick certainly needs defending these days. You hit it right on the button, young lady, when you wrote that "Christmas would be far too complicated for the younger set, who would not grasp it at all, if it weren't for Santa Caus, who gives them the spirit of giving."

How lucky you are to have been born into a family that makes the spirit of giving come true all year round. Your jolly fisherman Daddy and your warm and loving Mummy bring laughter and happiness wherever they are, and so do your brother and sisters and even good old Schuyler, your collie(?).

It is something to behold the Sibley household as Christmas draws nigh. Work on the fishing nets in the Rocky Neck studio is set aside, and the place becomes a regular Santa's workshop with all sorts of strange and wonderful "self-made" surprises under way.

And high up on the hill your big old-fashioned house just seems to palpitate with activity. Bevies of pretty decorations are turned out with paper and scissors and paste amid flights of carolling. As for the kitchen, a person has to stay clear and watch his step because Mummy sees to it that a perfect parade of goodies will march forth from the famous old wood stove until the very instant, almost, of Santa's arrival.

What a happy sight it is to drop by on Christmas Eve and find all gathered in the parlor before the crackling blaze, opening the gifts, and exchanging many a quip and loving glance.

Which reminds me, my dear: Did you know that many, many years ago, perhaps as many as a hundred, the tip-top of one of the high ledges overlooking Smith Cove, not far from your house, was known to one and all as Bonfire Rock?

Well it was, and the reason is that as long as anyone could remember it was traditional every Christmas Eve for the young people of East Gloucester to gather and light a bonfire on that rock which could be seen all over town — to make things so hot for St. Nick that he would have to come out of his hiding place.

Getting back to your letter — giving, just as you say, is the real spirit of Christmas. Santa helps to make it real for children, and people like the Sibleys help to make it real for everybody.

Christmas is a national holiday because there are more people in this country who claim to be Christians than anything else. But the Jewish people have their own celebration at this time, too. It is called Chanukah, the Festival of Lights.

It begins the evening after Christmas this year with the lighting of a candle. Then each day another candle is lit. It is a time of rejoicing, too, and the Jewish children receive gifts.

Therefore I don't think you have to be this or that or the other to be specially happy yourself and to make other people happier during this season, whether it's called Christmas or Chanukah or what.

As for Santa Claus, I doubt that he could care less as long as he can bring joy to homes and particularly to the children in them.

There is one thing about the celebration of the birth of Jesus and the jingling arrival of Santa that we all can agree about, don't you think? That is that this is a time for all the world to take hope again, to really believe that life can be better than it is for millions of people who are not as lucky as we happen to be by the accident of our births.

This is why it is a time for children to remind the grownups of some things. The future here in Gloucester belongs to you and your classmates at the Eastern Avenue and all the other schools, as you've been told so often.

But do they tell you that the biggest reason why we have so many problems in the world is that too many of us grownups have lost the hope and belief in something better that made our eyes sparkle when we were your age?

This thing that happens to so many of us when we leave our childhood behind goes by the long name of disillusionment, which is the excuse we use to give up or — as the youngsters who are half children and half adults say — to drop out.

The future belongs to you and all the other kids in this old fish town. Don't let anybody take it away from you by telling you that you're licked before you start.

Have a Merry Christmas, Marion, and give my hearty regards to the old gent with the whiskers if you should happen to see him first.

Sincerely yours,
Skipper Joe
December 15, 1967

Marion is now married, with a doctorate in biology, and teaches college in upstate New York.

45. 'TWAS A DICKENS OF A CHRISTMAS

ANOTHER CHRISTMAS HAS COME and gone, bless my soul, and Christendom is the better for it, isn't it? The snow lies even whiter on the ground. The childish eyes shine brighter. More wishes than ever have been granted.

The register bells jingled almost if not quite as merrily as was so prayerfully hoped for. And the church pews had their semi-annual dusting.

Yes, the Christian world is a happier and holier place today for having celebrated in a style that surely would have warmed His heart, on His Birthday.

And since we are blessed with so much more than enough love and joy to go around amongst ourselves, some of it cannot help but have spilled over into the rest of the world, and they are the better for it, too.

It is not a time for cynicism, or pessimism, the day after Christmas. No, nor yesterday, nor the night before either.

The last of the spirits, the Ghost of Christmas Yet to Come, you will remember, conveyed the frightened old man to the cemetery in the darkest hour of that Christmas Eve of long ago and pointed downward to the grave where on the stone was written his own name, EBENEZER SCROOGE.

Already that night Scrooge had achieved a lifetime of insight, and the lesson was clear. Said he to the Spirit, in a voice that trembled: "Men's courses will foreshadow certain ends, to which, if persevered in, they must lead. But if the courses be departed from, the ends will change. Say it is thus with what you show me!"

Well, Ebenezer Scrooge, of course, was humanity. Charles Dickens, an old-fashioned moralist, wrote "A Christmas Carol" 127 years ago and thereby, as G.K. Chesterton remarked caustically in his introduction to a new edition some years back, "struck in time and saved a popular institution while it was still popular."

Chesterton was making the point that Christmas in the England of 1843, just beginning to feel the crunch of the Industrial Revolution, was in danger of withering from pollution and degradation of the spirit. Dickens was a man of the people, and they listened to him, and just in time he dashed off his call for plum pudding and festiveness, and something more, and saved the Day, as Dr. Holmes would for Old Ironsides with, "Ay, tear her tattered ensign down!"

How mighty is the pen! "But if the courses be departed from, the ends will change."

If Dickens were to reappear in our midst today, as if led on himself by his Ghost of Christmas Yet to Come, what would he say of the institution he had saved?

What Christmases have come, and gone, in this century and a quarter, and what hath befallen the human spirit — the impoverished, degraded, polluted spirit of his fellows that moved this vain and human genius perhaps almost single-handedly to trigger a sort of reversal of those inhuman forces in a changing, revolutionized society that were mangling the fabric of life in a mash of machinery?

The human spirit moves, nay struggles on, Dickens would say, surviving even its Christmases. And he would peer about him through the smog, were he back with us today, and his eyes would water, and he would take a breath and cough and gasp: "I told you so."

"But if the courses be departed from, the ends will change." For it is not Christmas that works its magic, but Man.

December 26, 1970

46. Up from the sea on Sib's Hand-Cranked Marine Railway —⚓—

SPRING FITTING-OUT TIME IS HERE, and that means gearing up Captain Charles William Sibley's Hand-Cranked Narrow Gauge Marine Railway, Unincorporated, the smallest of the three on Rocky Neck.

Well, it was hand-cranked up til about six years ago; before that it was automated — mated with an auto, that is.

The Sibleys own an ample double-house on the harbor side and a studio on the Smith Cove side of the road at the west end of the causeway that connects the continent of Rocky Neck with the island of Gloucester.

Now and then someone wants to know why I don't write a book about the man. Simple. I wouldn't have him suspect there was anything more ulterior in my friendship than using his railway and workshop, borrowing his tools, taking advantage of his boat-carpentering expertise, picking his brain for Gloucester waterfront lore, and passing on an occasional Siblism to a reader.

Anyway, while a soldier in England during World War II this big young fisherman met and fell for an English soldieress, Margaret Bell. Back home recovering from serious injuries including the loss of sight in one eye (he was found with his bicycle in the road, a hit-and-run-victim and was in a coma for weeks), he wrote her: "I'll stake you over; if you decide not to marry me, I'll stake you back."

And so it came to pass, and they set up housekeeping with his folks in the two houses father George had wedded across Rocky Neck Avenue from his studio/shop. Pa was a wiry English shipwright who found work building schooners at John Bishop's yard on the shore of the since filled-in Vincent's Cove, and, as the fates decree in such matters, met Henrietta, an Ohio schoolteacher, in New York, where their only child was born.

Bill bought a sturdy old-time sailboat that father and son converted into the forty-odd-foot fishing dragger *Peggybell,* and signed on Tommy Morse, a compact young guy from over East Gloucester Square way who never wanted to do anything but go fishing. And the question inevitably arose: instead of grounding her out on the flats against the studio pilings for working on down in the mud at low water, why not build a little railway to haul her up on, high and dry, all tides of the day and night?

It happened that old Cap'n Jim Walen, who kept in touch with such matters, knew about a no longer used marine railway for hauling a private motor yacht in and out of its boathouse on Lighthouse Cove over at Eastern Point. An easy deal was made. Bill and Tom loaded this cameo utility on a float, towed it up the harbor to Smith Cove, and transplanted it on a set of ties buried in the primordial ooze alongside the winter workshop — summer studio formerly of A.W. Buhler and Theodore Victor Carl Valenkamph.

Question was, how in Sam Hill do we get old *Peggybell* or any other vessel of her heft up the track? Well, auto-mate it, of course!

They ran a steel cable low to the pavement between utility poles roughly across from each other on Rocky Neck Avenue, using this as a diagonal bridle for a standing double block attached on a straight line with the railway. Their rope tackle led through a running block on the cradle, back through the standing block and east along the side of the avenue to the rear bumper of Tom's Model A Ford. Harebrained maybe, but it worked; just watch out for traffic.

Until one morning. Tom had the old Ford in low, head-ing along the gutter, inching *Peggybell* up, when along comes a car, right out straight. Sib jumps out to wave it down, but not in time. It was Hal Fisher, the electronics man, on his way to the Big Railways on a Big Boat job.

From the low curb the cable was only a couple of inches off the street, twangy taut, but when it bounced back up from Hal's front tires it clipped off his muffler. Ole Fisher slammed on the brakes, came to a screeching stop, charged out of his car, looked at the setup, fixed the dumbfounded Sibley with an icy stare, strode back and picked up his muffler, threw it in the trunk, got back in, and roared on out of sight but not sound without ever a word.

Clearly this would not do. The railway was designed for *Peggybell*, max, and whatever workboat Morsie might be contemplating. Tom would become probably the most successful gillnetter in Gloucester. Bill was now concentrating on flatfish, observing with growing concern the indiscriminate catch that came up in the cod end with each tow, and learning firsthand about the effects on the fisheries of overfishing as well as pollution.

Self-taught, Sib was singularly knowledgeable about all aspects of fishing, and it was to the skipper of the *Peggybell* that marine biologists, fisheries experts and oceanographers were already turning for their inshore research trips east of Woods Hole. He was the first working fisherman in Gloucester to grasp the implications of resource management.

No, the matter of the lamppost was, well, stretching it a bit too taut under the circumstances. A technological leap was in order. And that is how an easy deal was made with John Alexander senior for the ponderous hand-cranked deck winch once employed in hoisting blocks of granite from the quarry wharves on the Back of the Cape to the long-retired stone sloop *Herbert,* dozing in the dock at John's Beacon Marine Basin.

The Stone Age Winch, in the Sib's double entendre, was planted for eternity at the railhead. Slow as Longfellow's mills of God, yet it ground exceeding fine. The massive gears turned the great drum by infinitesimal degrees, winding up the quivering steel cable pulleyed to the cradle and its burden, all set in motion by two pairs of arms wielding opposing cranks.

The whole works is kept smeared with the blackest of used crankcase oil. When applied with a brush every few years to the shingles of the adjoining studio as well, this "Sibco" doubles as a guard against the weather, not to mention the patina a recently Sibcoed shingle bestows upon the fabric when casually leaned against by the unwarned wearer of a Brooks Brothers tweed jacket.

Fleets of craft, work and pleasure but all pleasure in the process, have made the round trip on the Sibley Limited besides *Peggybell*, including my old 35-foot schooner *Bandit*. Many have been saved by the art and craft of the proprietor, and very few have ended up in the workshop stove.

At high tide you bring your boat up over the submerged cradle, center it with lines fore and aft, chock the cleverly hinged bilge trusses, and give the Sib a shout. He and Tom, if Tom's in from fishing, and maybe Georgie B (for Byard; there are other Georges) if he's on his lunch hour, leap with feigned eagerness to the cranks. Clank, clank,

clank, inch by quarter-inch we creak and shake up the track, of course attracting a curious knot of passersby.

"I am looking for men with keen, active, intelligent minds!" gasps the master mind of all this between huffs and puffs — "and strong backs!"

Invariably a few youthful sturdies have joined the gallery and spring to the fore. Will and his opposite reluctantly give way. Up the track we crawl as the keen, active intelligent minds redouble their efforts if the girls are watching, until we're able to leap dry-shod ashore and stride forward for the final triumphant fling at the

Captain Bill Sibley, son George, and the Stone Age Winch haul the dragger Peggybell, *daughter Annie in the bow. Rocky Neck, circa 1956*

crank that brings her home.

The brake is applied, the safety chain shackled from cradle to winch, and the chosen few retire across the street to Peter's (in the days when the senior Peter Anastas beamed at one and all across his lunch counter) for a collation on the owner of the vessel just hauled at such small cost and effort to him, with nary a demurrer save the gasping imprecations of each successive eager cranker who soon enough grasped the implications of the Stone Age Winch.

"Yes, we're getting a little older," declared Georgie B the Mechanical Wizard in 1967 as he lined up the old four-cylinder cement mixer engine, just acquired in an easy deal from Linsky's junkyard, with The Stone Age Winch and connected the drive chain. Sib and Tom and I almost heartily agreed.

So now Cap Sibley thrusts the garden hose into the water intake, opens the gas line, flicks the switch, fiddles with the choke, pulls the throttle, advances the spark, and gives a smart spin with the engine crank. He grunts, he sighs, he fiddles some more, cranks some more, mutters, cranks again, pulls at the

lobe of his ear, cranks, and after it gets good and damn ready the magneto comes to life, and the old thing sputters and begins to warm to the job. The flywheel gathers momentum, Will gives the visor of his cap a tug, throws in the clutch, chomps down on his cigar, and up she rises out of the sea.

And that's the way it is when the April or even the May sun climbs the vernal skies over Gloucester Harbor, and the boat fever strikes in down on the Neck, and it's the season once again to ease her onto Sibley's Hand-Cranked Narrow Gauge Marine Railway, Unincorporated.

March 30, 1973

One day, eight or nine years after this piece appeared in 1973 (I've enlarged it somewhat), Bill had posted himself alongside his faithful old winch to haul a boat. Now rather fully paunched to put it bluntly, he leaned over to tend something and the meshing gears caught his shirt in the midriff. Too late, he pulled back. The machinery grabbed his pants as well and commenced simply to consume them off his body, for he was a man of tremendous strength and was determined to pre-

serve his flesh, all the while shouting for help.

Help arrived on the double, ignorant of the workings of a cement mixer engine, and here is Sib, roaring instructions, the last remnants of shirt, pants, belt and finally drawers disappearing into the innards of old Stone Age.

After an eternity someone found the simple switch that grounded out the magneto, and the Winch clunked guiltily to a stop. As fast as he could, for even his abdominal amplitude had not escaped a nibbling, my old friend hurried across the street to Peggy's English Bookshop and burst in the door, clad in nothing but cap and shoes.

The mother of their five children, long accustomed with British aplomb to expect the unexpected from this original of originals, thought her old boy had finally flipped.

"Will, what on EARTH have you been doing?!!"

"Peg," he replied with that hand-in-the-cookie-jar look he employed when an event took an unexpected turn, "I got caught up in my work."

ON FEBRUARY 25, 1983, SIB DIED IN *his sleep. He was 64. Something in all of his pals went with him.*

47. ABOARD A GLOUCESTER BED HAMMOCK, DREAMIN' MY DREAMS

THESE SULTRY SUMMER EVENINGS when most anything is too much, I am inclined to just flake out on my Gloucester Bed Hammock with a cold can of something, crook one leg over the side for propulsion and drift off.

To my way of thinking, this old earth would be a better place if there were more Gloucester Bed Hammocks, most particularly if a few were slung from portico ceilings in Washington and Hanoi, Moscow and Peking, as seats for the mighty.

The Gloucester Bed Hammock gives the best of all three worlds. It is heaven-sent to be enjoyed right here and now, and it is comfortable as can be. It is balm for the restless soul, tonic for the flagging spirit, soother of the savage breast, a restorative for the mortal coil and a soporific for the sleepless psyche.

In short, it squares with

Dreamin', 1972

the Puritan ethic of the likes of myself by combining peace and unpretentious comfort with mild exercise. It is absolutely, though by no means painfully, functional in design and appearance. It is old fashioned . . . and it is a real swinging piece of furniture.

This contraption to which I have such an addiction in my

off moments consists of a few yards of heavy cotton duck such as they used to make sails out of, some wood battens, a handful of grommets, a few fathoms of cotton cord and manila ropes, a metal frame bedspring, a mattress, two stuffed pillows and the ingenuity to put them all together. It's a hanging, free-swinging bed, that's what it is, and for those who want more privacy or a lee against the breeze it comes with a canvas windscreen that can be unrolled and laced up along one side.

When I was a kid 40 years ago my grandmother had three Gloucester Bed Hammocks in her summer cottage at Riverview on the Annisquam River. Two hung on the southwest verandah, tawny and musty, like an ancient storm trysail that had weathered many a gale, which makes me think they must have been tanbarked. They always kept the windscreen rigged; that kind of hobbled them, and they were inhabited mostly by the older folks who were after more relaxation and less excitement.

The other Gloucester Bed Hammock at Grammy's hung right in the unplastered front room from the unpainted pine matched-board ceiling, mellowed nut-brown with the patina of age and salt air and the smoke from a thousand fireplace incinerations of the daily trash of the household, the dump being over on the other side of town.

Diagonally along one of the boards right overhead was a man's footprint. I'd lie there, swinging idly, and wonder about that footprint when I was supposed to be chipping away at my summer reading list for school. I suppose it's there yet.

This inside hammock had once been white duck, but generations of scrimy hands and feet had taken care of that. No windscreen. It was a free spirit, and when you got it swinging you knew you were going somewhere.

My cousins and friends and I would jump aboard, one at either end like streetcar motormen trying to go two ways at once, with a third amidships for ballast, and swing out. I think the whole house moved a couple of inches back and forth on its foundations when we got up to cruising speed, and when we really drove her on the home stretch it's a wonder that we never broke loose and took right off through the wall.

Depending on the fantasy of the moment, we'd line the pillows up along the sides and make a train out of it, choo-chooing along through unfriendly Indian country, or by piling them kind of aft we'd give her a pilot house and be a fishing dragger in heavy weather, the secret being to incorporate a sideways rolling motion into the pitch. A bit of this went a long way, and we'd be feeling pretty queasy as we headed back to harbor.

One trick was to leap on or off while in full swing, and if your timing was perfect on a spectacular athwartships oscillation you could pitch yourself through the air clear across the room. Needless to mention, such extravaganzas as piling chairs and a table on board for a go at circus acrobatics were vetoed — when detected.

The times in the old inside hammock at Grammy's that stick with me best, though, were the evenings of summer when I'd flop half propped against a couple of pillows that had that sea-salt smell to them, one leg over the side to give just an easy locomotion as desired, or even lazier, to slide down until my bare feet were flat against the canvas and keep it gently moving with a nudge from my toes on every backswing.

Then I'd gaze out the square of the window, through the open front verandah and over the dark forms of the trees where the fireflies sparked, away up the bends of Squam River and catch the friendly blink of Squam Light and hear the chug-a-chug of a dragger homebound from the Bay. And there'd be a cricket somewhere around the fireplace, sawing away when he felt like it, and the steady squeaky creak of the eyes in the hooks overhead as my bed swayed nonchalantly, and I'd turn my head and see the lighthouse flash on the opposite wall, and dream my dreams.

Well, that was 40 years ago, and then early in 1970 I discovered to my uncontainable joy that somebody was still putting out the Gloucester Bed Hammock. Way back when, the hammock was made and for all I know invented by E. L. Rowe and Son, the famous Gloucester sail makers. I have a promotional booklet put out by the Board of Trade in 1909 with their ad depicting "Rowe's Gloucester Bed Hammock" exactly as it was in my youth and exactly as I found it to be when I heard that D. F. Harris and Sons, the Gloucester sail and awning people, had come by the original patterns some time after Rowe went out of business.

And so they hauled one down from the loft and dusted it off. Same hammock I rode the rails and went to sea on except that foam rubber has replaced straw in the mattress.

It hangs now from another porch with a matched board ceiling (no footprint though), and it squeaks with every swing. And of a summer evening I don't mind flaking out with my head propped on a couple of pillows, giving the foot of it a little nudge on the backswing.

And I can look out the big window and catch the friendly flash of the Eastern Point Light, and spot a firefly against the brush, and hear a dragger chug-a-chugging up the harbor, and dream my dreams.

July 15, 1972